SEA
AND INVER

The Mediterranean Sea

LAWSON WOOD

NEW
HOLLAND

First published in 2002 by
New Holland Publishers (UK) Ltd
London • Cape Town • Sydney • Auckland

Garfield House
86–88 Edgware Road
London W2 2EA
United Kingdom
www.newhollandpublishers.com

80 McKenzie Street
Cape Town 8001
South Africa

14 Aquatic Drive
Frenchs Forest, NSW 2086
Australia

218 Lake Road
Northcote
Auckland
New Zealand

ISBN 1 84330 104 0

Publishing Manager: Jo Hemmings
Project Editor: Camilla MacWhannell
Editing and design: D & N Publishing,
    Marlborough, Wiltshire
Line drawings: Mick Loates
Cartography: Carte Blanche, Paignton

Reproduction by Modern Age Repro House
Limited, Hong Kong
Printed and bound in Singapore by Kyodo
Printing Co (Singapore) Pte Ltd

Acknowledgements
Many thanks to the many people and organizations who made this project possible and in particular: Lesley Orson; Jo Hemmings; Helmut Debelius; Dr. Elizabeth Wood; Professor Alexandre Meinesz and the University of Nice; Mark Busuttil and St. Andrews Divers Cove, Gozo; George Vella and Calypso Diving Centre, Gozo; Ian Pitchfork and Aquaventure, Malta; Mike & Agnes Upton at Maltaqua, Malta; Mike Mandale, Ramon Siliceo and Xalco Dive Centre, L'Estartit, Spain; Mark & Diana Davies, Valbonne, France; Igor Indjein from Golf Juan, France; Michèle Tourrette of Telemaque Plongee, Roquebrune, France; Fred Short and Rock Marine, Gibraltar; Photos Socratous and Cydive, Cyprus; Guido Schwengersbauer and Posejdon Croatia Diving Club, Croatia; Eurodivers, Zakynthos, Greece; Loisirs de Tabarka Dive Centre, Tunisia; Alf Chappell and the European Diving Centre, Turkey; Mansour and the Extreme Team Diving Club in the Lebanon; Hugh and Sardinia Scuba Tours, Sardinia; Marine Conservation Society; The Shark Group; Sea & Sea Ltd; Alan James Photography; Ocean Optics; Eastern Photovisual; Harlequin Worldwide Travel; Snooba Travel; British Airways; Air Malta; Go; Ryanair and Easyjet.

CONTENTS

The Mediterranean 5
External Features of Fishes 22
Identification Groups and Pictorial Guide to Families 22

PLANTS

- Seagrasses 26
- Algae 26

INVERTEBRATES

- Sponges 32
- Cnidarians 38
- Bryozoans 50
- Worms 54
- Molluscs 58
- Crustaceans 70
- Echinoderms 78
- Ascidians 82

FISH

- Sharks 86
- Rays 88
- Eels 90

- Pipefish 92

- Snipefish 92
- Lizardfish 92
- Anglerfish 94

- Scorpionfish 94
- Groupers 96
- Cardinalfish 98
- Jacks 100
- Barracuda 100
  - Grey Mullet 102
  - Drum 102
  - Damselfish 102
  - Goatfish or Mullet 102
- Picarel 104
- Smelt 104

- Bream 104
- Wrasse 108
- Parrotfish 112
- Dragonet 112
- Gurnard 114
- Blenny 114
- Stargazer 118

- Weaverfish 118
- Gobies 118
- Codfish 122
- Flounder 122

OTHER VERTEBRATES

- Turtles 124
- Dolphins 124

Glossary 126
Index 126

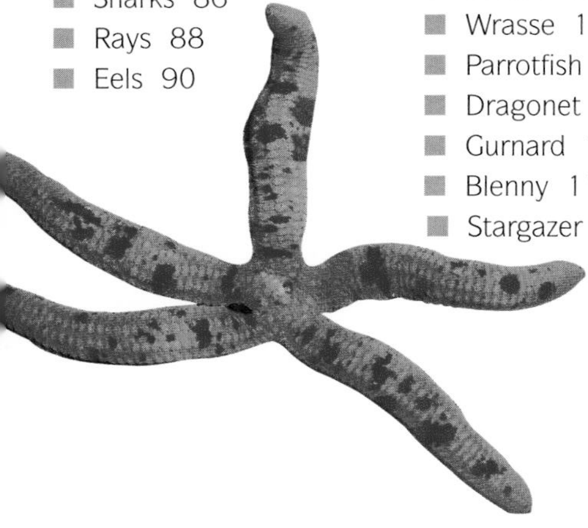

THE MEDITERRANEAN

Known as the 'Cradle of Civilization', the Mediterranean Sea is now set in a massive flooded depression in the earth's crust formed over millennia. This vast expanse of water is almost completely landlocked, stretching from the Straits of Gibraltar in the west to the coasts of Turkey, Syria and Israel in the East. The Mediterranean both links and divides three continents, Europe, Africa and Asia. The varied depths of this basin also support varying communities of marine life and although all of the species found in the Mediterranean contribute to the whole, we shall only concern ourselves with what we can see, practically and with the least effort, whether it be from swimming, snorkelling, scuba diving, or even fishing and sailing.

With water temperatures that never drop below 10°C, the Mediterranean has remained fairly isolated over the years and has evolved a distinct ecosystem only troubled by man's intrusion. The region is complex and diverse in its geography, history and climate, with much of what we know and see only coming from the northern shores and around many of the islands.

Known for its very singular climate, the present shores of the Mediterranean were roughly formed five million years ago; however, it took early form over twenty million years ago when the western shores were still closed and the eastern end was still linked to the vast primeval Tethys Sea. As the years passed, Africa slipped anticlockwise, Arabia split from Africa forming the Red Sea and the eastern stretches of the Mediterranean also became landlocked. Whilst this continental movement was progressing, the land areas were gradually 'crumpled' up forming a ring of mountains which now comprise the Sierra Nevada, the Alps, the Atlas Mountains, the Dinaric Alps, the Rhodope Mountains, the Akhdar Heights and the Taurus Mountains. Over the subsequent two or three million years, the now-landlocked Mediterranean filled and evaporated several times as the earth's crust shifted, often leaving gigantic salt marshes and mud pools where dinosaurs once roamed.

As far as can be agreed between scientists, about five million years ago, there was a massive cataclysmic earthquake which opened up the Gibraltar sill, and the Atlantic Ocean poured into the basin taking almost a century to fill. Today, this connection to the Atlantic Ocean is still very evident and water pours into the Mediterranean at approximately 4km/h (2.5mph) in a layer from 75 to 300m (250–1,000ft) deep. This sea water gradually evaporates and the heavier, more salty water sinks and eventually flows back out through the Straits of Gibraltar, taking around eighty years to replenish the water column.

This has had several knock-on effects, one of which is the reduced amount of plankton to be found in the Mediterranean and what plankton there is, quite often flows back out into the Atlantic in the deeper ocean currents. This ultimately produces less marine life, but also clear water in general. As always, there are notable exceptions and wherever there is a large river run-off there will be periodic algal blooms which reduce visibility. Rough seas in shallow areas also contribute to poor visibility, but in general one should expect underwater visibility of about 30 to 50m (100–165ft).

Colourful corals can be found all around the Mediterranean coastline and offshore islands.

A Sea of Seas

Although not truly one sea, but several joined together, the individual seas are defined by the surrounding land masses formed when the earth's crust collided. There are two principal areas known as the Eastern and Western Mediterranean roughly separated by the mid-ocean ridge which runs from Italy to the African coast. The Alboran Sea is found in the west, connecting to the Algerian Sea or Balearic Basin between Algeria, Sardinia, Spain and France. The Gulf of Lyons and the Ligurian Sea stretch along the southern coast of France, the Tyrrhenian Sea surrounded by Corsica and Sardinia to the west, Italy to the east and Sicily to the south. The two most famous of the Mediterranean's seas are the Adriatic and the Aegean; it is on these seas that the history of mankind spread from the old to the new worlds. The Gulf of Trieste, in the northern area of the Adriatic Sea, is formed with Italy on its west, Croatia and Albania to its east; further south the Ionian Sea

Corfu, in the Greek Islands, is a popular tourist destination.

separates the southern coasts of Italy and Sicily with the Maltese islands to the west with Greece and its many islands to the east. Separating Greece and Turkey is the Aegean Sea which is connected to the Black Sea in the north-east by the Dardanelles, Sea of Marmara and the Bosporus. In the eastern reaches can be found the Levant Sea bordered by Turkey and the islands of Crete and Cyprus to the north and Syria, the Lebanon and Israel to the east, with Egypt and Libya to the south. The Ionian Sea and the Levant Sea are roughly divided by a shallow stretch of water sometimes referred to as the Libyan Sea. The Ionian basin is the deepest part of the Mediterranean at 5,121m (17,000ft). In Egypt, of course, can be found the man-made Suez Canal, opened in 1869, which links the Mediterranean with the Red Sea.

Man's Impact

Bounded by mountains, man has made his impact mainly on the narrow coastal plain some 20 to 30km (13–20 miles) wide and in some areas of southern France and northern Italy, man has literally carved a space from the mountains themselves. With the one notable exception along the North African coast, virtually all of the Mediterranean's population can be found along this narrow coastal strip and its associated islands. Much of the coastal plain was dominated by mosquito-infested swamps and history tells of the canal and irrigation systems which drained the swamps and irrigated the land for cultivation, thereby virtually eradicating malaria. Much of the original forest has been cut down by man, leaving a rather sparse scrubby landscape.

The Mediterranean basin and surrounding countries have some 350 million people; 135 million of them live around its shores. Economic and industrial growth has resulted in vastly increased pollution levels. The need to feed this increasing population, and its annual tourist trade of over 100 million visitors, has put further strain on the sea and its marine life. Much of the original coastline has been irrevocably changed by man's expansion and development with yacht marinas, harbours and housing developments. Small countries such as Monaco have now lost some 75 per cent of their original coastline. The Mediterranean Sea is undoubtedly one of the world's most

Diver and Dusky Grouper *Epinephelus marginatus*.

now a new threat, placed once more at the door of one of the world's most influential men who brought the sea and its awareness to our very homes through the media of television, engineering and photography.

Jacques Yves Cousteau was one of the primary men involved in the invention of the aqualung, that singular device which has allowed man's (shallow) exploration of the seas to expand into a worldwide sport. His Marine Institute in Monte Carlo in the principality of Monaco was at the forefront of marine exploration and the understanding of the environment. In 1984, whilst Jacques Cousteau was still a director of the institute, a small patch of an alga called *Caulerpa taxifolia* was discovered beneath one of the windows of the marine institute. This alga, a native of Martin Bay, Brisbane, in Australia was reared as an aquarium alga for tropical fish and was first reported in Europe (in Stuttgart Aquarium) in 1969. The alga, although certainly not genetically modified, had inevitably undergone some genetic mutation in the closed environment of the institute's aquaria. It would appear that an aquarium and its contents were emptied out of the marine institute's windows and this alga, hitherto unknown in the Mediterranean, started to grow.

This act, originally accepted by the authorities, was soon dismissed as it was thought that the alga could not survive in the northern Mediterranean's colder water temperatures during the winter months. The director of the institute, Professor Doumenge, stated that this was purely a temporary phenomenon. However, as the alga started to spread, the act was denied by the French authorities as being some import either owing to global warming or even a Lessepsian visitor via the Suez Canal from the Red Sea.

It was soon discovered that not only were there no known predators of this alga, but that it spread through fragmentation. This spread was entirely owing to man's influence again, whereby ships' anchors and chains and fishermen's nets were inadvertently dragged through it, breaking off the leaves and stems: and when the offending equipment was put back into the sea in another section of the coast, the alga immediately started to grow. The Côte d'Azur was soon dotted with this rapidly spreading alga. Professor Alexandre Meinesz, a biologist from

threatened seas, owing solely to the increased demand on its natural resources primarily through pollution from homes, industry and intensive agricultural methods. Fortunately, the fresh seawater influx from the Atlantic has managed to stave off much of its demise, at least for the time being.

Killer Algae

Even whilst the major problems of pollution are now being taken on board by the Mediterranean's surrounding countries, the impact on the local sea environment is actually very small considering the size of the Mediterranean Sea. Small areas such as around Venice and the northern Adriatic, sections of the Greek coast and parts of Tunisia are under increased threat owing to tourism demands, but this is usually on a temporary seasonal basis. The marine life does regenerate in these areas with seasonal changes. However, if man's impact was not enough in altering and destroying the coastline, there is

Typical reef with Chromis *Chromis chromis* and starfish.

discovered by divers off Cape Martin on the Italian border and this initial area now covers over 3ha. The number of reported cases increased tenfold in the next year. In 1992, the alga was discovered in Majorca, Italy and Corsica, covering an approximate area of 420ha. By 1997, it was found in Croatia around Split, Messina in Sicily, the island of Elba and now covers 4,700ha. At the same time 300ha of small patches of *Caulerpa taxifolia* were found at Sousse in Tunisia and by 2001, this area had expanded to over 13,000ha. Whenever new sites are found by divers or reported by yachtsmen or fishermen, the report is verified by the university and added to the mapping of the now dubbed 'Killer Algae'.

Outbreaks of *Caulerpa taxifolia* have since been discovered off San Diego in California and in New Zealand. UNESCO have been informed of the catastrophic effect that the alga is having on the future of the Mediterranean, but as yet, the French authorities have still not come up with the cash or the personnel to try and extract the weed from the sea. One way of killing the plant is by spreading a large black plastic sheet over the affected area and then treating the alga with chlorine. This also kills off all other types of life, but at least the regeneration over time by Mediterranean species is preferable to *Caulerpa*.

The alga is not only overtaking all local marine life; as a by-product of its growth, it creates a mud residue, further smothering this fragile ecosystem. A few small nudibranchs have been discovered that feed on this alga; but nowhere near the numbers needed to halt the spread. A few small bream are starting to eat the alga, however, the plant is so toxic that it will take several generations of fish before they are immune. Then there is the problem of human health, should these toxic fish appear on the fish market.

However, early indications do show that the plant can be killed off by various methods and these trials have been successful in California and some areas of Spain. The sea slug *Elysia* is known to eat the alga exclusively and several types of copepods also thrive on the alga. It is hoped that with continued monitoring and the immediate response by all Mediterranean government agencies, this ecological disaster in the making may be averted.

the University of Nice, was called in to assess the probable damage and subsequent spread of the alga. After 18 months of intensive research, Meinesz concluded that there was no way of stopping this ecological disaster. Six years later, Professor Meinesz stated that *Caulerpa taxifolia* was like a metastasizing cancer whose spread could not be halted and which could eradicate all life. He said 'The water of the Mediterranean does not drop below 10°C; at this temperature, the alga is in stasis and can survive quite happily for over three months; at 15°C, the alga starts to grow quite rapidly; at 20°C, *Caulerpa* grows at over 3cm (1in) a day'. One of the most ironic factors is that Monaco promotes itself as a leading country in marine conservation, yet 75 per cent of its coastline is totally destroyed by development and now a further 90 per cent of the seabed is totally wiped out by *Caulerpa*.

In just five years, the 1m (3ft 3in) patch had already grown to one hectare. By 1990, it was

The Habitats

Corals are not overly evident in the Mediterranean and owing to the changing water temperatures during the year, there are no true coral reefs, made up of the stony hard corals more associated with tropical coral reefs. As such, the rocky 'reefs' are generally composed of ancient limestone blocks from some past age when corals were more prevalent in the Mediterranean. These are now colonized by a living mantle of a mixture of small corals, sea fans, sponges, other cnidarians and various algae. Rocky coastlines and small islands have become encrusted with marine life and many species are found only in the Mediterranean. Much of the classification of the world's marine animals has come from the early observations made in the Mediterranean.

The habitats are as diverse as they are in any specialized environment and, although there are some very deep basins in this sea, we shall only concern ourselves with the veneer, which we are able to see whilst visiting this ancient sea whether by scuba diving, snorkelling or rock-pooling.

Rockpools

These areas found after a receding tide are a mini oasis of life, often containing creatures, which are able to withstand both a rapid change in salinity (after heavy rainfall in a shallow pool) and differences in water temperature (such as at the height of the summer when the water temperature in shallow pools can rise alarmingly for the 6–8 hours before it gets covered by the advancing tide once more).

Sand

Typically, worm casts of marine worms are seen in most places. The tracks of marine snails and other creatures are also found, and this region is home to flounders, skate and rays. Many burrowing creatures also make this habitat home, such as starfish, urchins, anemones, eels and gurnard. Many beaches on the east coast of Spain, Syria, Lebanon and Israel, and much of North Africa, are some of the best beaches in the Mediterranean and their pure white sands are wonderful. Many islands have huge sand dunes formed over millennia as wind-blown sand piles up on the shore.

Mgarr Ix-Xini, Gozo.

Mud

Deeper sea-beds and those affected by river run-off build up a muddy seabed owing to the amount of detritus, which gets washed into them during periodic winter storms and heavy rainfall. Burrowing animals such as various molluscs, sea pens, mud crabs, brittle starfish, fireworks anemones and burrowing anemones are typical of this habitat and are all excellent photographic subjects.

Rocky Shores

These offer a firm substrate base for algae and other sedentary organisms to attach. The particular selection of marine life found will depend on the type of rock. Some soft rocks can be bored into whilst other glaciated granitic rocks only have a slight scattering of animals as there is nothing for them to get a firm grip on. Exposed locations will always be beaten badly by adverse weather conditions and this factor will also determine the types of marine life found. Chitons, sea

(*Left*) The Blue Hole, Dwejra, Gozo.

(*Above*) Diver exploring a cavern.

urchins, limpets and barnacles are perhaps the most common rocky shore inhabitants.

Rocky Cliffs

Submarine cliffs are well known for their colourful fields of jewel anemones, underhanging ledges covered in parazoanthids, huge forests of red and yellow sea fans, tube worms, sea squirts and other more sedentary creatures. But it is more the nature of the habitat which is appealing to divers, as there are often caves and caverns associated with these cliff faces, that when combined with a deep vertical wall, undoubtedly increase the enjoyment of the dive.

Caves and Caverns

Wherever the coastline is made up of a mixture of ancient limestone or sandstone and where geological upheaval has shifted the earth's rock strata, caves and caverns are found. Some of the most spectacular are found in north-eastern Spain, the Balearics, Corsica and Sardinia, Malta and Gozo. Huge vertical clefts cut through headlands and tunnels harbour marine species which might otherwise only be found in very deep water. Creatures which favour these dark conditions are sponges, slipper lobsters, small shrimps and precious red corals.

Shipwrecks

Well, we all know the attraction of such edifices, but these are important habitats, quite often found in areas which would be otherwise rather poor in marine life. Wrecks provide an important holdfast for soft corals, sea fans, sponges, sea squirts, algae and are also home to many different species of commercial fish. Many of the wrecks are, however, in deep water and quite often in areas of strong tidal currents. This not only limits the diver intrusion (which personally I feel is a good thing), but these wrecks would not have the same amount of marine-life colonization without those limiting factors.

Piers

The most obvious of the man-made structures which abut the seashore, the piers and break-waters found around the Mediterranean are quite often the only shore access on many stretches of coastline, as man has irrevocably changed the original coastline in the pursuit of more living space, commercial enterprise and tourism facilities. These structures have evolved over the centuries as boat traffic has altered in shape, size and frequency of visits. When all else fails and you want a reasonable dive in fair conditions with a super abundance of marine life, then the piers and breakwaters will give you an abundance of marine life, usually including octopus, cuttlefish, anemones, sponges, mussels and simply tons of other invertebrates which live on or in the encrusting algae.

Posidonia

Fields of *Posidonia oceanica* (Neptune Grass) are very typical of most Mediterranean habitats and are 'indicators' (indicating the presence) of clear, clean, oxygen-rich water. Posidonia meadows are important nurseries for fish and shellfish and are home to many other associated species.

The presence of Posidonia meadows on the seabed are a vital and indispensable habitat.

Caulerpa

Fields of the newly introduced *Caulerpa taxifolia*, on the other hand, are seen as a plague along the southern coast of France, Monaco, Corsica and Majorca. This introduced species is spreading uncontrolled through the Mediterranean, smothering indigenous species of Posidonia and other beneficial algae. The presence of Caulerpa means that all of the (local) marine life species and habitats are under severe threat of extinction.

Tidal Rapids

Common in a number of localities between various islands, tidal rapids are home to sponges, algae and other invertebrates which feed on the swiftly moving plankton passing on their way four times each day. Here the seabed is a mass of life and is considered a high impact zone.

PROJECT AWARE

Ten ways a diver can protect the Aquatic realm (produced by the Professional Association of Diving Instructors – PADI):

- Dive carefully in fragile aquatic ecosystems, such as coral reefs.
- Be aware of your body and equipment placement when diving.
- Keep your diving skills sharp with continuing education.
- Consider your impact on aquatic life through your interactions.
- Understand and respect underwater life.
- Resist the urge to collect souvenirs.
- If you hunt and/or gather game, obey all fish and game laws.
- Report environmental disturbances or destruction of your dive sites.
- Be a role model for other divers in diving and non-diving interaction with the environment.
- Get involved in local environmental activities and issues.

An evening dive.

Reef Conservation and the Tourist

Marine conservation is not new in the Mediterranean. Most of her bordering countries have specific marine parks, many of them over twenty years old, providing important nursery areas for many different groups of fish. Commercial fishing is still concentrated at the perimeter of these marine parks, as the protected areas can only support so much marine life, allowing the 'overspill' to be fished.

Unfortunately, many important habitats and breeding areas have already been severely depleted and in some cases totally destroyed. Offshore islands have generally been spared from man's commercial activities. However, the coastline bordering the Mediterranean has been under threat since man first inhabited her shores. Many offshore reefs and rocky shoals have been overfished. The catches of fish in general have been reduced to alarming levels and traditional fisheries have collapsed in many areas.

The traditional tuna trapping or *mattanza* (from the Spanish word for 'slaughter') in Sicily and Sardinia still occurs each year as the common tuna *Thunnus thynnus* migrate from the Atlantic to their spawning grounds in the Mediterranean. These catches are now affected by Asian longliners which catch huge quantities of tuna and other large pelagics without reference to any authority in the Mediterranean.

More insidious fishing methods have also affected the Mediterranean's fragile ecosystems.

Aquaculture has grown alarmingly, as the ever-increasing population and tourists require feeding. Some fish farms require huge amounts of fish meal subsequently contaminating the surrounding seas with nutrient-rich waste products. Grey mullet fisheries in Egypt have been successful, as these fish are vegetarian and also feed on detritus.

Mussel and oyster culture is responsible for the introduction of a further sixty species of algae from the Japanese archipelago, all of which have been released into the wild from the seedling stocks imported from the country. Many people depend on the sea for their livelihood, yet even these are constantly under threat from the more commercial aspects of fishing for the mass market.

Thankfully, most countries now accept that a successful tourist industry relies on strict conservation policies and the protection of natural wetlands and fisheries. For this industry to succeed and prosper, tourists also have to be aware of the impact which even they can make on small areas, therefore education at all levels is vitally important. Membership of conservation agencies is always a clear step into the understanding and protection of the marine habitats.

Endangered Species

A number of marine species in the Mediterranean are threatened, principally due to the acts of man. Although pollution will always head up one of the main causes for the loss of a species in a specific area, it is so localized that this is rarely the

Old Tuna anchors, Tarifa, Spain.

Fish waiting for market, Tarifa, Spain.

case, as more strict antipollution measures have also helped clean up much of the coastline. The dangers are much more direct owing to the physical nature of the cause. Sport spear fishing has wrecked havoc on local inshore populations of large fish with a more sedentary nature such as the grouper. Overfishing and the systematic plunder of fishery resources have resulted in massive reductions in brown meagre, tuna, grouper and crayfish. Trophy catches such as the giant Mother of Pearl File Clam or the collection of living skeletons (precious Red Coral) for the jewellery trade have all had a detrimental effect on the ecosystem.

Local destruction and degradation of seagrass meadows with the construction of new ports and marinas has led to a far more insidious threat from increased tourism, where repeated use of ships' anchors, devastating use of fishing gear and increased (local) pollution have all led to the loss of many *Posidonia* meadows, as they are unable to reclaim lost areas. Couple this with the alarming rate at which *Caulerpa taxifolia* is covering the northern Mediterranean shores, and it can be argued that all of the Mediterranean species are under threat.

Red Coral Corallium rubrum
Divers still lose their lives each year as they search increasingly further into deeper water and caverns for this small fragile coral. Used exclusively in the tourist jewellery market, the brilliant red branches of this exquisite coral are a delight to see underwater and are thankfully protected in a number of areas.

Mother of Pearl Pinna nobilis
The Guinness Book of Records records the giant Mother of Pearl Pen Shell as the second largest shell in the world (after the Giant Clam). This species of mussel can exceed 1m (3ft) in height and is traditionally found in *Posidonia* seagrass meadows. Known to grow for over twenty years, they are collected by trophy hunters and also used in the jewellery trade.

Crowned or Long-spined Sea Urchin Centrostephanus longispinus
Sea urchins have long been regarded as a delicacy in the Mediterranean and the Long-spined Sea Urchin has been collected for generations. However, a virus has wiped out much of the Mediterranean population and although it is quite common in the eastern Mediterranean, it is considered quite rare elsewhere, but has been recorded as far west as Gibraltar.

Dusky Grouper Epinephelus marginatus
The local grouper population in the Mediterranean has been decimated by spear fishermen. Fairly sedentary in habit and often curious of nature, grouper have been an easy target for spear fishermen over many years. Malta and Gozo, Turkey, the Greek Islands, eastern Spain, Italy and southern France have all suffered from this. However, areas such as the Medas Islands in northern Spain, northern Sicily and the areas between southern Corsica and northern Sardinia are home to very healthy populations of large grouper.

Posidonia Sea Grass Posidonia oceanica
Posidonia is found off all Mediterranean coasts from depths of 0 to 40m (0–130ft). It is a flowering plant, and not an alga. It is home to myriad marine creatures and an important fish hatchery, the plants actually anchoring the seabed. Growing at only 3cm (1in) per year, to replace the vast meadows of Posidonia which have been lost owing to the construction of coastal marinas would take 3,000 years! Replanting programmes are ongoing in many coastal countries.

Seahorse Hippocampus spp.
The Seahorse is just one of many species affected by the loss of Posidonia meadows and coastal construction. The loss of the habitat is perhaps the largest problem facing these enigmatic and curious fish, but there are other factors which also threaten their existence, such as indiscriminate fishing methods and the Asian pharmaceutical interest, whereby over twenty million seahorses are sold throughout the world annually.

Monk Seal Monachus monachus
Near extinction, the Mediterranean Monk Seal has been hunted mercilessly by fishermen over the last fifty years as it was seen as the singular largest threat to fishermen's livelihood. Now severely restricted to a few small desert islands

The Seahorse *Hippocampus ramulosus* is an endangered species, threatened by severe habitat loss.

modern binomial system of nomenclature (i.e. genus and species) was developed by Linnaeus and dates from publication of his *Systema Naturae* in 1758 and subsequent years.

The scientific (Latin) name of an animal comprises the name of the genus to which it belongs, conveniently written in italics, or even underlined in some texts. This first name always has a capital letter and is followed by the specific or trivial name which is always spelt with a small letter, e.g. *Posidonia oceanica* (Neptune Grass). Once you get into the habit of using the proper scientific names you soon find how easy it is and how good it is for describing species in a common language used by enthusiasts.

Making Choices in Marine Conservation
When booking a holiday, research the area first and use only diving schools which are involved with their local marine parks and conservation initiatives.

Contact the appropriate conservation agencies to see if there is specific information on the areas that you may want to dive.

Ask your tour operator if they have an environmental policy and if they contribute to marine conservation societies.

Make sure that dive shops and operators explain their specific conservation policies before the dive or snorkel, as this will undoubtedly help your awareness and lessen your impact on the marine environment.

Follow the example of other conservationists and use biodegradable shampoos, dispose of your litter appropriately, use fresh water sparingly and try and further the conservation message.

Souvenirs
Collection of marine souvenirs is prohibited in most areas, so respect all local and international laws.

The collection of empty beach shells may well seem innocent, but these shells may be used by small blennies as nesting sites, or by hermit crabs looking for a new home. Be careful in your selection.

All corals and turtle products are protected under CITES (the Convention on International Trade in Endangered Species) and can be bought and sold only under licence.

between Greece and Turkey, early initiatives in marine conservation appear to be working. However, with a restricted gene pool, the future of Monk Seals in the Mediterranean is bleak. The seals are also found in Madeira and a few isolated pockets of Morocco.

Classification and Nomenclature
You will note that in this guidebook to the Mediterranean, many species names of marine life are given in both the common and Latin scientific name. Common names are given wherever possible, but with so many different countries around the borders of this sea, it is almost impossible to find a common name to suit all species. The scientific name describing the nomenclature of a particular animal is very important. When diving in various parts of the world, or even in the same region, you may come across several different names for the same creature. This can be confusing. Scientists prefer that when identifying or describing a particular animal, you use its scientific or specific name.

The correct naming of a species is very important for your own log book records and is essential to scientists and marine biologists studying flora and fauna now and in the future. The

Red Hermit Crab *Dardanus calidus* at home.

Never buy marine curios, as they will probably be from another area of the world which is under even more threat and where the fishing methods used in the collection of the species may well be suspect.

Sea Stingers of the Mediterranean

As far back as written records began, man has recorded the plight of his fellow creature being stung by one or another of the denizens of the deep. Aristotle first accurately described the stinging properties of stingrays and jellyfish in 350 BC. The Greek poet Oppian wrote how the barb of a stingray could kill a tree and, on that same note, Pliny, describing the stingray, wrote in the *Historia Naturalis*: 'So venomous it is, that if it be struchen into the root of a tree, it killeth it: it is able to pierce a good cuirace or jacke of buffe, or such like, as if it were an arrow shot or a dart launched: but besides the force and power that it hath that way answerable to iron and steele, the wound that it maketh, it is therewith poisoned.'

Venom in most cases is used purely for defensive purposes. As a working underwater photographer specializing in marine life studies, you quickly learn that if the creature that you are approaching does not swim away, then it must have some other form of defence. These creatures include small coelenterates and jellyfish, the tiny bristles of fire worms, and the pointed, modified tips of fins from various fish, anemones, sea urchins, starfish, molluscs and corals. In general terms, stinging mechanisms found around the mouth parts are for offensive reasons and stinging parts found along the back and tail are defensive in origin.

Different creatures have different types of toxins and potency. Most cause localized effects such as numbness, irritation or paralysis; others kill nerves, blood cells or attack muscles and affect internal organs. Most have a cumulative effect and cause several problems at the same time. In certain circumstances, these toxins can even cause death in humans. Around fifty deaths each year are attributed to sea stings of some nature.

As already mentioned, the most common stingers are jellyfish. These come in a vast army of different sizes and potency. All are members of the same superfamily which includes corals and anemones. These creatures are primarily offensive stingers. Their stinging mechanism is in the form of a hooked barb fired by a hydraulic coiled spring. These barbs are called nematocists and are held inside a trapdoor until they are released by touch or chemicals in the water. The barbs are hollow and filled with toxins which are released as soon as the stinger penetrates its victim. The primary aim is paralysis, before ingestion. Most jellyfish sting, but few are dangerous.

When seasonal changes are in their favour you can encounter the Portuguese Man-of-War *Physalia physalis* in tropical waters. These are highly toxic and continued exposure to the stinging cells may require hospital treatment. Whenever the conditions are favourable for Luminescent Jellyfish *Pelagia noctiluca*, there is always the chance of swimming beaches being affected. It is the almost invisible microorganisms in the water column which can cause skin irritation, so swimmers should wear protection such as a wet suit or the new style of Lycra skin suit. There are local remedies available for stings, but acetic acid (vinegar) is as good as anything. In cases of severe stinging, medical attention will be required. Closely related are the anemones, hydroids and corals, all of which have a surprisingly large number of harmful representatives. Most anemones will not do any harm to the much thicker skin on your fingers, but many can inflict quite painful 'burns' on the softer parts on the inside of your arms or legs. Species such as the Berried Anemone *Alicia mirabilis* has warty tubercles all over the stem of the anemone; each 'berry' is armed with lethal

Diver and Cassiopeia Jellyfish *Cothyloriza tubercolata*.

nematocists. The more common anemones use their barbs to hook and paralyse prey which swim inadvertently within their 'sticky' grasp.

Hydroids such as the Sea Nettle *Pennaria disticha* have harmless-looking, feather-like plumes which can inflict a rather nasty sting on the softer areas of your skin if you brush up against them.

Even the most innocuous-looking sea creatures often have a hidden battery of stingers just waiting for something to rub against them. A few sponges have tiny calcium spicules which when rubbed against actually have a very similar effect to that of fibreglass rubbed against the softer parts of your skin. This can cause severe irritation, rashes and sores.

Fire worms *Hermodice carunculata*, although quite cute in appearance, should never be handled. These attractive, small worms have clumps of white hairs along their sides which display bristles when touched. These bristles easily break off in the skin causing a painful burning feeling and intense irritation. Although they are not deadly, stings will require treatment, principally with hot water and vinegar.

Perhaps one of the species we most associate with stings are members of the stonefish and scorpionfish families. There are no stonefish in the Mediterranean, but there are several species of scorpionfish, all of which are armed with a mild,

toxic venom in the modified hollow spines found at the tips of the dorsal fins. These are not considered dangerous but care, as always, should be taken to avoid the spines on the top of the dorsal fin. Inadvertent stinging can be helped by placing the affected area into very hot water.

Other stingers in the fish world are the stingrays as previously mentioned. If you do encounter stingrays at close quarters, you must never attempt to grab hold of the tail or sit or stand on a stingray's back, as the stinging mechanism is located in the tail. Any undue force on the creature may cause it to spring its tail forward in a reflex action, thus erecting the spine and causing serious damage. There are also species of electric ray found in the Mediterranean, which should be avoided. Weaverfish *Trachinus draco* like to inhabit shallow coastal areas and lie partly buried in the sand. They have a venomous spine on top of the dorsal fin and, although not lethal, it can cause extreme discomfort when stepped on. Similar species are stargazers *Uranoscopus scaber*, which have two venomous spines, one situated on each side behind the gill covers.

Not all stingers are large and obvious; quite a large number of molluscs also have stinging mechanisms. Nudibranchs, for instance, eat stinging hydroids and anemones and have the ability to store the stinging nematocists of their prey in their own tentacles. When attacked by predators, they are able to utilize the stored nematocists in defence.

Sea urchins and starfish are the last and most obvious group of sea creatures that seem to lie in wait for unwary and clumsy humans. Thankfully, with good buoyancy control and using cameras and lenses, which allow them to photograph these spiny creatures, divers are now able to avoid most brushes with these animals. The spines of a number of sea urchins can be poisonous. Even if not, they can puncture the skin – even through gloves – leaving painful wounds which can become septic. Although much rarer now in the Mediterranean (owing to an epidemic which almost wiped out the entire population) is the Long-spined Sea Urchin *Centrostephanus longispinus*. This urchin should be avoided as the spines are quite brittle and easily broken off in the flesh. Made of calcium, the spines in the flesh should dissolve after a few days. Deeply embedded spines may leave permanent scarring and patients may have to be treated for shock. Treatment includes rubbing the juice and pulp of the pawpaw, or even urine!

Most wounds to the unwary and uninitiated are caused by ignorance, as mentioned earlier. If the creature does not retreat from you, exhibits bright colours or moves into a defensive posture, then you can be fairly certain that it has a defence mechanism which can harm you. For those unfortunate enough to encounter some of the pelagic stingers of the sea, such as tiny microscopic jellyfish, all the advice that you have will never prepare you for the agony. It is recommended at all times never to scuba dive in just a swimming costume. You must always wear either a full wet suit or at the very least, one of the modern Lycra-type 'skin suits' for overall protection. If you are cautious and careful with your buoyancy, you should be able to gain a new understanding and appreciation on these much maligned 'stingers of the sea'.

Diving Areas
Gibraltar
Starting from the extreme west and working along the northern shores of the Mediterranean, the northern 'Pillar of Hercules', or Gibraltar as it is more commonly known, is at the entrance to one of the world's natural crossroads. It is here that the incoming current from the Atlantic Ocean mingles with the denser Mediterranean Sea creating a unique combination of flora and fauna. The 'Rock' as it is known, is home to several superb wrecks dating back to Napoleonic times, with the best of the wrecks being located off the breakwater and dating from the Second World War. These wrecks are home to a huge amount of marine life including sea fans, cucumbers, schools of anthias, nudibranchs, octopus and cuttlefish.

Spain
Much of the southern Spanish coast is very similar in topography and species diversity to Gibraltar. As you travel north-east towards the French coast there are a number of marine protected areas, with good diving and excellent marine life to be found at Al Muñequa and Fuengirola. The most famous of all the protected areas is the Medas Islands off the coast near the resort of

Gibraltar, at the entrance to the Mediterranean, is home to a huge diversity of marine species.

Medas Islands, Spain, are a protected marine preserve.

Estartit. These small rocky islands have been protected since the early 1980s and have absolutely huge concentrations of fish, including grouper, Sea Bass, bream, sardines and mullet. The mainland coast is carved with hundreds of gullies, caves and caverns, many of which travel several hundred metres underground and are home to slipper lobsters, colourful sponges, spiny lobsters and sea hares.

Balearics
The Spanish dependency islands of Formentera, Ibiza, Majorca and Menorca all have excellent diving, with many fine diving schools. The small

island of Cabrera is undeveloped and is now a national park. The entire area has a similar feel to Malta and Gozo, with deep caverns, huge burrowing anemones, plenty of algal turf being grazed by wrasse, but few big fish. The best diving in Majorca is along the mountainous west coast between the ports of Polense and Andratx and there are huge schools of barracuda at the tip of Dragonara Island. Pont D'en Gil cavern in Menorca is popular with divers due to the ancient stalactite and stalagmite deposits underwater, testimony that this cave was once on dry land, before the Mediterranean was flooded.

France
There are a number of marine parks all along the southern French coast starting with the nature reserve of Cerbère-Banyuls just north of the Spanish border. Very similar to the geology of Estartit with many sea caves, the reserve is supported by the Arago Oceanographical Laboratory located at Banyuls-sur-mer to the north. The reserve is noted for its Dead Men's Fingers and precious red corals. Near Toulon, the island of Porquerolles is administered by the French National Trust and has many interesting wrecks nearby. The Côte d'Azur has excellent diving around the offshore islands near Cannes, Cape Juan and Cape Antibes with some superb walls and interesting topography.

Monaco
Known as the home of the famous Oceanographical Institute supported by Jacques Yves Cousteau, Monaco still promotes itself as a leader in

Monaco is believed to have played a central role in the introduction of the so-called 'Killer Algae' *Caulerpa taxifolia*.

world conservation policies, yet it has lost 75 per cent of its natural coastline due to development. Monaco is now seen as being directly responsible for the introduction of *Caulerpa taxifolia*, which is endangering the entire Mediterranean.

Corsica
Cap de Scandola on the north-west coast of Corsica is set in the heart of a marine park which is dominated by huge tortured red volcanic rocks that plunge into the sea. Difficult to get to, the diving in the marine park is dominated by fields of red and yellow sea fans. Off the south-east coast can be found the Lavezzi Islands Nature Reserve which has been protected since 1970. The islands, of granite formation, are renowned for their friendly populations of large grouper.

Sardinia
Sardinia is under the protectorate of Italy and on the other side of the Strait of Bonifacio can be found the twin island nature park of Maddalena Island, also favoured by fish watchers. South of this small archipelago can be found the Gulf of Aranci at Capon Figari, where large concentrations of the Giant Fan Mussel *Pinna nobilis* can be found, some of which are almost 1m (3ft 3in) tall. Off the north-east coast can be found the spectacular cave and cavern formations of Nereo Cave at Capo Caccia. There are also a number of scenic wrecks to be explored along the east coast of the island.

Italy
Near Santa Margharitta at San Fruttuoso can be found the underwater sculpture of the 'Christ of the Abyss' placed by Guido Galletti in 1954. A copy of this statue can be found in the Pennekamp State Park in Florida. Commemorating the life of Cressi Sub founder Egidio Cressy, the statue is in the centre of a fine marine park which is home to thousands of damselfish. The island of Giannutri midway down the west coast of Italy has a couple of fine wrecks and nice sheltered bays. The 'Nasim II' and the 'Anna Bianca' are both in deep water, but are surrounded by thousands of anthias. The next group of islands to the south include the island of Ponza, where the wreck of the 'LST349 MK.III' lies. Sunk in 1943, the ship is an eerie reminder of the last World War. On

Canoeists exploring the Mediterranean coastline.

nearby Ventotene Island can be found the wreck of the 'Santa Lucia', which also dates from 1943, but is a much better wreck for marine life.

Sicily
Bordering two major sea areas, Italy forms part of the ancient land bridge which once split the Mediterranean. Not widely known for its conservation policies, Italy has made more obvious steps in recent years with the tiny island of Ustica, just 36 miles off the coast of Sicily, facing Palermo. The tip of a subterranean volcano, the island is known for the huge amount of Sea Rose *Sertella beaniana* which can be found everywhere. Large colonies of Red Sea Fan are also evident. On the east coast, near Catania, can be found the marine reserve of Aci Trezza. Founded in 1992, the reserve is studied by the University of Catania, which has counted more than 300 species of algae within the park's boundary. The islands are said to be the historical 'Cyclops Islands'. Legend has it that the island is actually the colossal stones flung by the giant Polyphemus at Ulysses' boat.

Croatia
Located bordering the north-eastern Adriatic, the islands off the coast of Croatia have been a sailor's delight for years. Now divers are exploring beneath the waves, particularly off the island of Korcula and although the area has been over-fished for many years, the invertebrate populations are high, with many different hermit crabs and nudibranchs. Large sponges, feather starfish and Red Sea Fans are symbolic of the diving off Korcula. Great White Sharks have been spotted near Istria, following the tuna migrations. There are several sites which have ancient amphora as well as wrecks from the Second World War including a fairly intact German submarine.

Greece
The Greek Islands are said to be the cradle of civilization, and there are countless numbers of historical monuments and ancient wrecks to testify to this fact. Diving has been fairly restricted until recent years, owing to the sensitivity and importance of so many treasures still to be found underwater. There are now a number of commercial centres on a few of the islands and although the fish life is scarce, the topography is interesting.

Crete
Separated from Turkey by the Sea of Crete, this ancient Mediterranean island has some

interesting diving around its rocky shores. Best for diving is the western shore, which is less touristy. Nearby Chania has a large area of ancient amphora, now covered in an algal turf. There are large schools of bream and wrasse as well as interesting caves and caverns.

Cyprus
Diving is very popular in Cyprus, particularly around the Paphos region, with a number of diving schools having excellent reputations. The most famous wreck in Cyprus waters is that of the 'Zenobia' which sank in 1980. This 172m (570ft) wreck is a must for all divers visiting the island. The Akamas Peninsula is now earmarked as a marine park and the Akrotiri Fish Reserve near Limassol is very popular.

Turkey
South-eastern Turkey has some superb diving, especially those dives around the popular holiday resorts of Fethiye and Marmaris/Icmeler. Although it is not noted for its fish life, the huge sponges, octopus and other invertebrates more than compensate. The region is also dotted with

Mosaic of a fish at Pompeii, dated AD 79.

ancient shipwrecks, sea caves and caverns, perfect for exploration. Turkish divers also know of a certain area where you can encounter Dusky Sharks *Carcharinus obscurus*.

Syria
There is little knowledge of diving off the coast of Syria, but from accounts by Turkish divers the topography is very similar, with an interesting mix of fish coming up from the Red Sea. Diving here would have to be done by special permission and then only by boat.

Lebanon
A new Mediterranean country on the diving scene, there are a number of good wrecks in Lebanon, mainly dating from the civil war that shook the country in 1975. However, the country is also known to be home to small numbers of Ragged-toothed Sharks *Odontaspis ferox*.

Israel
There is some inshore diving to be found on the Israeli Mediterranean coast, but it is fairly restricted and generally on some not too ancient wrecks. These are all well colonized now by different algae and small anemones. Fish life is interesting, as there are a few migrants from the Red Sea to be found.

Egypt
The Egyptian coast was not known for its diving until some archaeology researchers found ancient remains off the harbour wall in Alexandria. These ancient sphinx, obelisks and statues

Chromis or Damselfish *Chromis chromis* in Paradise Bay, Malta, enjoy shallow coastal waters all around the Mediterranean.

Common Dolphins riding a bow wave off the coast of Tunisia

included in UNESCO's list of *Reserves of the Biosphere*. The rare Giant Limpet is found here as well as local groups of dolphin. The National Institute of Marine Sciences and Technologies, which was founded in 1927, is involved in continuous research on the islands. Founded in 1980, the second reserve includes the islands of Galite and Galiton off the northern Tunisian coast and consists of one main island and five smaller ones. Of granite origin, unique in Tunisia, the islands are renowned for the Posidonia meadows, crayfish, large grouper and precious red corals. Once home to the Monk Seal, it is hoped that a few solitary individuals may make the islands home once more.

are surrounded by damselfish and bream with a mix of fish and algae from the Red Sea. The area is quite unusual and will be open to mass market tourism shortly.

Libya

Newly opened for tourists, diving is still in its infancy, but early reports state that the offshore reefs and wrecks are pristine. Much of the larger inshore fish have gone, but there is a large invertebrate population.

Tunisia

The islands of Zembra and Zembretta were declared a national park in 1977 and are

Algeria

Little is known about the Algerian coastline, but there are tales of excellent wrecks from various political conflicts, sunken cities and good marine life to be explored.

Morocco

Owing to constant political changes in the country, there is little scuba diving done. However, several operators from Gibraltar and southern Spain do occasionally cross the straits to dive some of the offshore reefs and islands. These are known for large grouper, lots of sea fans and a wide mix of Atlantic marine life.

KEY TO SYMBOLS

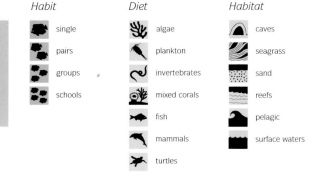

This key describes the symbols that appear at the head of each species description. The symbols give a quick guide to the habit, diet and habitat of each species.

Habit
- single
- pairs
- groups
- schools

Diet
- algae
- plankton
- invertebrates
- mixed corals
- fish
- mammals
- turtles

Habitat
- caves
- seagrass
- sand
- reefs
- pelagic
- surface waters

EXTERNAL FEATURES OF FISHES

This diagram illustrates the main structures of a fish referred to in the species descriptions.

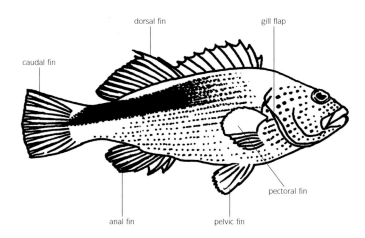

dorsal fin

gill flap

caudal fin

pectoral fin

anal fin

pelvic fin

IDENTIFICATION GROUPS AND PICTORIAL GUIDE TO FAMILIES

Colour varies greatly between fish species, therefore it would seem an ideal means of identification. However, even within species, colour varies according to sex, age, region, season
and surroundings. For this reason, body shape is a much more reliable means of identification. The following outlines represent all types of fish likely to be encountered in the Mediterranean. Those sharing similar characteristics are grouped together for initial identification.

RAYS AND SHARKS

Carcharhinid sharks pp.86–88

Lesser Spotted Dogfish & Nurse
Hound pp.86–88

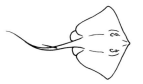

Stingrays pp.88–90

Electric Ray p.90

REGULAR-SHAPED FISH SWIMMING CLOSE TO OR ABOVE REEF

Sea Bass p.96

Mullet p.102

Picarel p.104

Sand Smelt p.104

Bream pp.104–108

Wrasse pp.108–112

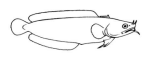

Codfish p.122

COLOURFUL REGULAR-SHAPED FISH CLOSE TO REEF

Seaperch p.96

Groupers p.96

Combers p.98

Cardinalfish p.98

Brown Meagre p.102

Chromis p.102

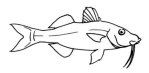

Striped Mullet p.102

Parrotfish p.112

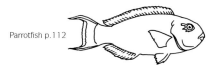

ELONGATE FISH CLOSE TO OR ON REEF SURFACE

Conger Eel p.90

Serpent Eel p.90

Moray Eel p.90

Pipefish p.92

Lizardfish p.92

Dragonet p.112

Blennies pp.114–116

Triplefins p.116

Stargazer & Weaverfish p.118

Gobies pp.118–120

SILVERY, TORPEDO-SHAPED FISH

Blue Runner p.100

Jacks & Amberjacks p.100

Barracuda p.100

IRREGULARLY SHAPED FISH

Seahorse p.92

Snipefish p.92

Anglerfish p.94

Rockfish & Scorpionfish p.94

Gurnard p.114

Flounder & Turbot pp.122–124

Plaice p.122

SEAGRASSES

Seagrasses are the only flowering plants in the sea and there are three representatives to be found in the Mediterranean. The flowers are tiny and obscure, appearing in the spring and early summer. Seagrasses anchor the seabed and spread by their root-like rhizomes.

1 CYMODOCEA
Cymodocea nodosa

Less common than Posidonia, the leaves of Cymodocea are grey-green in colour, reach only 50cm (1ft 8in) and have lacy edges, joined in tufts at the base and which grow from a thin rhizome. These plants prefer warm, calm waters and a fine surface sediment, and when in flower, they appear at the tip of the stem, but are rarely seen.

2 HALOPHILA
Halophila stipulacea

This is a Lessepsian migrant from the Red Sea and colonies have reached as far west as the islands of Malta, Gozo and Sicily. It has a rounded top to the 4cm (1½in) long, green blade and patches spread by a common root system with each new plant forming around four to six leaves. Other than its invasive nature into other areas of the Mediterranean, indications are that it does not compete with other Mediterranean seagrasses. But ultimately, all migrants are competitive and studies are still underway.

3 NEPTUNE GRASS
Posidonia oceanica

By far the largest concentration of seagrass found around the Mediterranean shoreline is Posidonia. Growing on sand and detrital bottoms, huge meadows can be found in localized areas and the species is an indicator of clear, clean water. Growing very densely, the leaves are up to 1m (3ft 3in) long and are an important habitat for all manner of marine life. The detritus from Posidonia is often washed up on wind-swept beaches where the algal debris collects and forms small seagrass balls.

ALGAE

Algae are incredibly widespread and diverse, with several hundred species being recorded in the Mediterranean, and more being discovered each year as migrants from other, more distant seas. Some are single-celled, living in the tissue of some hard coral polyps, others are multicellular, spreading over rocky surfaces. Many grow in tufts and some are so delicate, it is hard to imagine that they are in fact algae. Most species have specific predators, which browse on them, such as fish, sea urchins or snails. Algae can be split into three groups depending on their pigmentation. These are green, red and brown algae, most of which have relatives in other oceans of the world.

GREEN ALGAE

4 CHLOROPHYTA or MERMAID'S CUP
Acetabularia mediterranea

This unmistakable alga consists of clumps of thin green or white stalks topped with a thallus of a light green, rayed disc hardened by encrusted limestone. Umbrella shaped, it grows around 8cm (3in) tall with the disc being around 1.2cm (½in). In the growing season, it is preyed upon by various wrasse and bream species which eat the tops, leaving many empty stalks. Large clumps are concentrated on a stone or rocky substrate. It is quite often found on the lower shore and can grow as deep as 30m (100ft).

1 Cymodocea

2 Halophila

3 Neptune Grass

4 Chlorophyta *(below)*

1 COMMON CAULERPA
Caulerpa prolifera
This indigenous species of *Caulerpa* is still fairly common around the Mediterranean, particularly in southern and central areas where its cousin *C. taxifolia* (*see* below) is not as rampant as it is in the north. The two species have similar ways of spreading over all substrata by way of a common robust stolon or stalk. *C. prolifera* has wide branching blades protruding perpendicularly into the water. The blades reach over 15cm (6in) long and can be as broad as 13cm (5cm). *C. prolifera* is also very common in the Caribbean and is one of the species favoured by marine aquarists.

2 CREEPING CAULERPA
Caulerpa racemosa var. *occidentalis*
This is another highly invasive species, originally thought to have come through the Suez Canal from the Red Sea. However, indications are that the species is actually Australian in origin. Interestingly, *C. racemosa* is very prolific in the Caribbean and is located as far north in the Atlantic as Bermuda. It is also common in the Pacific and is used as a food source by Polynesians, who eat it raw with grated coconut and coconut milk. This alga spreads by means of long stolons. Its racemous rhyzoids point downwards and photosynthesis occurs in the clustered aggregations, which reach around 5cm (2in) in height. Bright green, with rounded lobes to each branch, this species appears to be both warm- and cold-water tolerant, occurring from 5m (17ft) to over 50m (165ft) depths.

3 KILLER ALGA
Caulerpa taxifolia
First introduced accidentally in 1984 in Monaco, this virulent alga has leaves that are small and paired, with the new growth being a pale green or even yellow. With no natural predators in the region, it is growing at such an alarming rate that the entire Mediterranean is at risk. It spreads from a single stalk, and the enzyme in the alga is toxic. Leaves can be from 6–65cm (2½in–2ft 2in) long and in 1m² (11 sq ft) of seabed an individual plant can have a stolon of over 3m (10ft) in length, with over 200 leaf fronds; in total, over 220m (240yd) of plant with 8,000 leafy fronds weighing 12kg (26lb)

have been found in 1m² of new *Caulerpa* meadow. *Caulerpa taxifolia* is very similar to *Caulerpa sertularoides*, which is often used in salads in the Philippines and is not in the least bit toxic.

4 FINGER CODIUM
Codium vermilara
Noted by the small clumps of 'fuzzy' fingers, this alga has a common root stalk and branches widely at its base to form many small rounded clumps of stalks. Quite often coated in a filamentous, slimy alga, Finger Codium is grazed on by a few species of nudibranch. This species enjoys aerated, shallow water conditions where wave surge and high light are present.

5 PURSE CODIUM
Codium bursa
Unmistakable rounded shape in various shades of green. Growing up to 40cm (1ft 4in) in diameter, as it gets older, the more uniform spherical ball develops a central depression. Found singularly or in small groups of various sizes on a rocky substrate, the exterior of the alga can get rather scruffy in appearance and quite often has other species of algae adhered to its surface.

6 SEA CACTUS
Halimeda tuna
Very similar in formation to *Halimeda* species found in the Caribbean, the Sea Cactus is made up of a series of distinct small rounded discs approximately 10cm (4in) long, which are joined together by a narrow strand. Coloured from a pale brownish-green to a brilliant green of new growth, the plant resembles the terrestrial 'Prickly Pear Cactus'. Often found under overhangs, it prefers shaded or deeper water conditions.

7 SEA FAN
Udotea petiolata
Typically fan-shaped with a convoluted, rounded edge, attached to rocky surfaces by a short peduncle. Quite often, there are darker green growth lines over the leaf which can grow up to 10cm (4in) high and during reproduction, the outer edge is tinged white. Growing in clumps and widely spread out over rocks, this alga is photophobic, preferring shallow light-filled, warm water. It is found in depths from 5 to 10m (17–33ft).

1 Common Caulerpa

2 Creeping Caulerpa

3 Killer Alga

4 Finger Codium *(above)*

5 Purse Codium *(left)*

6 Sea Cactus *(bottom left)*

7 Sea Fan *(above)*

RED ALGAE

1 RHODOPHYTA or ROUGH CORAL MOSS

Corallina elongata

Red or pale-pink seaweed made up of calcified parts loosely connected into a feather-like shape. Whilst growing, the new growth may appear lighter in colour than the stem. Often growing through other species of algae and small sponges, the tips of the 'feathers' are quite often all that you may see. However, it can also grow to form quite dense carpets of algae. Preferring shallow water, the fronds are 2–6cm (¾–2½in) long. It is able to resist rough seas and moderate pollution. This alga, when dried, was formerly used medicinally with other red algae for the treatment of intestinal worms.

2 JANIA

Jania rubens

Similar in structure to *Corallina elongata*, but much paler and thinner, *Jania rubens* comprises a large clump of calcareous and jointed fronds, which branch off dichotomously. The reproductive organs are in the form of a swelling at the joints and difficult to see. Growing from 1.5 to 4cm (½–1½in) in diameter, the rosy red alga forms circular clumps in shallow water and is quite often associated with numerous other algae which it tends to colonize.

3 STONE WEED

Lithophyllum lichonoides

Sometimes referred to as footpath alga or 'trattoirs', Stone Weed is strongly calcified and is common in surface waters where it forms a developing rim or cornice around shoreline rocks. The growth is determined by tidal movement and the cornices can be quite wide. Wherever it occurs in deeper water, it can be found on rocky bottoms in areas of strong tidal movement. Coral-like, with numerous hard and flattened fronds, it is purple in colour with white or pink new growth lines at the edges. It is very tolerant of wave action, preferring shallow water where it can become exposed at low tide. Similar in shape to *Pseudolithophyllum expansum*,

the individual parts of this alga grow to around 7cm (2¾in) and fuse with other, similar-sized parts to form a large 'reef-like' structure.

4 SEA ROSE

Peyssonnelia squamaria

Bright and colourful, the Sea Rose is brownish-red in colour and each part forms a small fan progressively getting larger as the fan grows out in petal-like formations. Pale yellow at the base of each petal, striated lines grow stronger in colour as they expand to the outer rim. Often appearing almost luminescent underwater, each rose may grow as much as 10cm (4in) in diameter and is often associated with a brilliant green alga. This colourful species prefers low light conditions either at the entrances to caves and caverns or on poorly illuminated hard rock bottoms where its range can extend to over 50m (165ft) depth.

5 SEA MAT

Pseudolithophyllum expansum

The sea mat is quite distinctive in shape and colour form, being a pale purplish-pink with a light outer rim. This very hard coralline alga encrusts large areas of poor light and is found on most rocky substrates from shallow waters down to over 60m (200ft). The growing edge of the alga can be deeply convoluted and is one of the contributory alga, which forms the Mediterranean reefs, cementing detritus, algae and rock together.

6 RED SEAWEED

Sphaerococcus coronpifolius

This species is particularly common in most coastal regions of the Mediterranean. Dark ruby red in colour and forming small clumps widely branching from a single stalk, these seaweeds prefer well-aerated, light-filled, shallow water. Quite often, wherever there has been damage to the rock surface by anchor or boat groundings, this alga is one of the first to take hold. Extremely opportunistic, it is not uncommon for entire rocky surface areas to be dominated by this quick-growing alga.

1 Rhodophyta

2 Jania

3 Stone Weed

4 Sea Rose

5 Sea Mat

6 Red Seaweed

BROWN ALGAE

1 PHAEOPHYTA or FORKED RIBBONS

Dictyota dichotoma

This is a delicate alga, the green chlorophyll masked by brown pigments, changing to a brilliant iridescent blue at the outer edge of its tips. Usually only growing to around 15cm (6in) high with dichotomously branching, ribbon-like fronds 2–12mm (1/10–1/2in) wide. With no mid rib to support the alga, it wafts in whatever current assails it. Fragile in nature, it is easily broken apart or knocked off its rocky base sand. Quite often found washed up on the shore.

2 SEA FERN

Halopteris scoporici

Widespread on all well-illuminated rock surfaces in central and eastern Mediterranean regions, the Sea Fern grows to around 15–20cm (6–8in) tall and has a thick, dark brown (almost black), single stalk branching to dense feather-like tufts which are rough in texture. Found in all depths, this alga is often overgrown by other species.

3 PEACOCK'S TAIL

Padina pavonica

Calcareous in nature, the fronds have a parchment-like feel to them. Each frond is flat and fan-shaped, changing to become funnel-like as it matures. Coloured light brown to white, it has darker, horizontal, striped growth lines. Tolerant of some freshwater run-off, it is quite often found on jetty slipways and pilings. Enjoying sunlight and warm calm waters, it is rarely found below 20m (66ft).

4 COMMON SARGASSUM

Sargassum vulgare

Sargassum weed can grow up to 1m (3ft 3in) in height and is widely distributed around the Mediterranean. It is fast growing and attaches to a rocky substrate. It has long, crinkly fronds with short, lateral, leaf-like structure branches, interspersed with small air bladders. It will tolerate some pollution and if broken free from its rocky base, the alga survives quite happily on surface waters buoyed by its air bladders. It provides a home and shelter for many small pelagic creatures.

SPONGES
Phyllum Porifera

Sponges are sessile animals, simply constructed with a single-body cavity with large exhalant pores and smaller inhalant openings lined with special cells called choanocytes, through which nutrient-rich water is passed. The exhalant tube is usually located at the highest point of the animal to allow for waste water to be carried away more efficiently. Sponges have no internal organs. Yet despite their simplicity, they are very successful organisms and are found worldwide in all different habitats. The hard structure of the sponge contains small calcareous or siliceous spikes or spicules which support the sponge. From an ancient class of animals, sponges are often difficult to identify as they change shape to suit their environment. In very exposed locations, sponges will be flattened, often covering large areas of rocky substrate. In calm sheltered conditions, many sponges grow quite spectacularly with large branching arms and delicate formations.

5 SPIKY SPONGE

Acanthella acuta

Relatively common, but only growing in small clumps in fairly shallow water, this sponge is often found on wrecks where it enjoys a firm holdfast. Obvious by its spiky shape, growing out over 25cm (10in), this orange sponge is variable in shape with obvious large oscula set back into the body and often has a rather fuzzy appearance.

1 Phaeophyta

2 Sea Fern

3 Peacock's Tail

4 Common Sargassum

5 Spiky Sponge

1 YELLOW TUBE SPONGE
Verongia aerophoba
Enjoying a rocky substrate in fairly shallow water from 5 to 25m (17–83ft), this bright yellow sponge is tinged with a symbiotic blue algae which quite often makes it look greenish or brown in colour. It forms small clumps with large, finger-like tubes approximately 3cm (1¼in) in diameter and up to 12cm (4¾in) long with an obvious exhalant opening at the end of each tube.

2 YELLOW BRANCHING SPONGE
Axinella damicornis
Often mistaken for *Acanthella acuta*, the Yellow Branching Sponge tends to be low forming with irregular outcrops of exhaling tubes. Almost lemon-yellow in colour, with a slightly 'fuzzy' appearance, this small sponge is rough in texture, and it prefers shaded areas, rarely growing below 15m (50ft) and only 10cm (4in) in height.

3 BRANCHING TUBE SPONGE
Axinella polypoides
Quite often found in muddy pockets on the lower rock substrate inside caverns, this columnar sponge, yellow or orange in colour, forms tree-like branches, which are cylindrical in shape. Depending on the surge quality of the water, this sponge may develop many small branches, or only one or two very long branches, growing up to 1m (3ft 3in) in length. Quite fragile, it can be easily damaged. Of the three large and similar species of *Axinella*, this species is recognized by its lack of tuberculous growths and generally it tends to have longer more cylindrical branches. *Axinella canabina* has many small, more-jagged, irregular branches rising vertically from a single stalk and *Axinella verrucosa* is fairly smooth and cylindrical, but also is comprised of many small branches and projections. The branches of *Axinella polypoides* are often so long that they get too heavy to be self supporting and drape themselves over the rocky substrate.

4 POTATO SPONGE
Chandrilla nucula
Particularly widespread in most areas of the central Mediterranean, this species is especially resistant to surge and rough seas as well as being tolerant of mild pollution from sewage. Resembling small, brown, new potatoes, this sponge only grows to a maximum size of 2cm (⅜in) and forms small patches on hard rock. Enjoying full sunlight, it is located on the tops of rocks and in shallow water to a depth of around 7m (23ft).

5 CLATHRINA
Clathrina coriacea
Rarely found in depths of less than 10m (33ft), this golden-yellow honeycomb sponge is only 3cm (1¼in) in height, but grows extensively over large areas. It prefers shaded areas and is common in caverns and under overhangs. Constructed of many small tubules, which link and weave together, it forms a raised pad, which quite often hangs down from cave walls. Looking somewhat like a lump of small netting, the exhalant valves or oscula are found at the ends of the interlocking tubes. A similar species, *Clathrina clathrus* is white in colour and is also found in both the Mediterranean and Atlantic. Clathrina is commonly associated with large colonies of the tunicate *Dendrodoa*, with which it interleaves, creating a marked colour contrast between the white and yellow of the sponge and the red of the tunicate.

6 BORING SPONGE
Cliona viridis
In varying shades of yellow and green, this species is probably much more common than originally thought, as its small size is so easily overlooked by marinelife observers. Looking like a series of excavated holes in the top of limestone rocks, the Boring Sponge has many inhalant and exhalant holes lined with calcareous spicules to trap organic matter. This sponge bores deeply into the soft rock and forms large colonies, the large holes of which are quite often used as refuge by small crustaceans or gobies.

1 Yellow Tube Sponge

2 Yellow Branching Sponge

3 Branching Tube Sponge

4 Potato Sponge

5 Clathrina

6 Boring Sponge

1 OYSTER SPONGE
Crambe crambe

The Oyster Sponge is quite common and found in fairly well-lit waters from a depth of 5 to 30m (17–100ft). Commonly associated with Thorny Oysters and other sedentary bivalve molluscs, this brilliant red encrusting sponge covers the outer shell of the bivalve. Ridged by raised oscula found along the exhaling channels, the colonies grow from 10–20cm (4–8in).

2 BREADCRUMB SPONGE
Dyscidea fragilis

Forming large mats of over 1.50m (5ft) in low light conditions, principally under overhangs or in caverns, the Breadcrumb Sponge is a uniform grey in colour tinged with light purple. This sponge forms many raised oscula and is quite unmistakable from any other species.

3 BLACK SPONGE
Ircinia spinosa

Particularly common in central and eastern Mediterranean regions, the Black Sponge grows to approximately 20cm (8in) in diameter and is a low encrusting species found on the tops of well-illuminated rocky surfaces in all depths.

4 LOBED SPONGE
Oscarella lobularis

Commonly found in caves and caverns, this fleshy demosponge has neither spicules or spongin. Forming large sheets over 10cm (4in) thick, it shies away from natural sunlight. Often forming large interconnected tubes pale cream in colour with brownish tips, this sponge can cover large areas of cliff wall or overhang and will colonize rocks and algae.

5 PINK CAVE SPONGE
Petrosia ficiformis

This common sponge is found in most cave and cavern situations and can cover large expanses of cavern wall in long, sometimes connecting, lobes. With highly visible oscula, the colours are variable and will be a combination of peach to grey/white and sometimes purple. This is a favourite food species of the Spotted Doris nudibranch *Discodoris atromaculata*, seen opposite.

6 ORANGE SPONGE
Spirastrella cunctatrix

One of the more common sponges found in the Mediterranean, the Orange Sponge grows over rocky walls and covers most other organisms. Bright orange in colour with quite obvious channels that run over the body leading to the oscula, it is often mistaken for *Crambe crambe*, growing over a much wider area, often taking over a rocky wall.

7 GREEK BATH SPONGE
Spongia officinalis

Lacking calcereous spicules, the Greek Bath Sponge has a complex structured skeleton of spongin fibres making it extremely flexible. A light pink or uniform grey in colour, this sponge is collected commercially for sale as a bath sponge. The oscula are sparse but conspicuous, being slightly raised from the textured body. Common in caves and areas of low light from shallow water to over 40m (130ft).

1 Oyster Sponge

2 Breadcrumb Sponge

3 Black Sponge

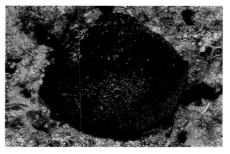

4 Lobed Sponge *(above)*

5 Pink Cave Sponge *(right)*

6 Orange Sponge *(above)*

7 Greek Bath Sponge *(right)*

1 LARGE ENCRUSTING SPONGE
Suberites domuncula
This is a large sponge developing irregular mounds and spheres with obvious oscula. It can grow to over 1m (3ft 3in) wide and 7cm (2¾in) thick. Quite hard and leathery in texture, it has three different types of spicules in its formation. It is quite often found growing on a Hermit Crab's shell, where it eventually dissolves the shell, creating a new secondary home for the Hermit Crab. This allows for the crab's growth pattern to get larger, without the need to change shells.

2 PURSE SPONGE
Sycon ciliatum
A quite distinct small sponge with a singular ovoid or spherical shaped tube around 7.5cm (3in) in length. It has a single, large oscula at the top surrounded by a stiff, spiky collar. Preferring shallow water and found in beds of mixed algae, this is an annual species, releasing its larvae in the spring.

CNIDARIANS

This is a large and fundamentally simple group of animals, widely distributed and seemingly totally diverse, in such a wide array of forms that they are not obviously related to one another. This family (phylum) formerly known as Coelenterata, includes true hard corals, soft corals, sea pens, sea fans, anemones, sea firs (hydroids), zoanthids and jellyfish. They come in two different forms, either as an attached polyp or a free-floating medusa.

All of the species are radically symmetrical without a right or left side. They have a single body cavity and a single terminal opening, usually surrounded by one or numerous rings of tentacles. It is these tentacles in various forms and adaptation which group the family together. Each tentacle is armed with stinging cells, cnidocytes, containing nematocysts. Nematocysts consist of small capsules which contain a smooth or barbed thread coiled inside. Used for defence or aggression and for catching prey, these stinging cells may also be found on other parts of the body. The toxins released when these 'harpoons' are fired may be powerful enough to cause a severe sting.

The typical shape is that of the anemone type with a single mouth, ringed with tentacles, with which the animal stings, stuns or captures its prey, to be drawn into the mouth and thence to the single, sac-like body cavity. Waste matter also exits through the mouth. Most cnidarians reproduce sexually, releasing floating larvae which inhabit other areas of the ocean. Some species split or bud to produce new polyps which remain attached thereby increasing the size of the colony, whilst others release free-floating eggs and sperm which are fertilized in open water, producing medusa which eventually settle onto the sea bed.

HYDROIDS

Commonly referred to as 'Sea Firs', hydroids usually live attached to rocky substrates and have a rather complicated life history. They are often mistaken for plants or algae. They form delicate fern or feather-like groups and can be quite profuse in certain areas. During sexual reproduction, they produce a free-swimming, tiny jellyfish called a hydromedusa. Although most hydroids have tiny polyps, they pack powerful stings and contact with them should be avoided.

3 SEA FERN
Aglophenia spp.
Difficult to identify specifically, *Aglophenia* spp. are typical of the feather type of formation, with each 'fern leaf' reaching around 20cm (8in) in length. Unbranched, the side 'shoots' are opposite each other and form two vertical rows. The male gnophores tend to congregate along the stem, at no set intervals. Very common on the tops of rocks, it is often overlooked and can sting the softer parts of your skin.

1 Large Encrusting Sponge

2 Purse Sponge

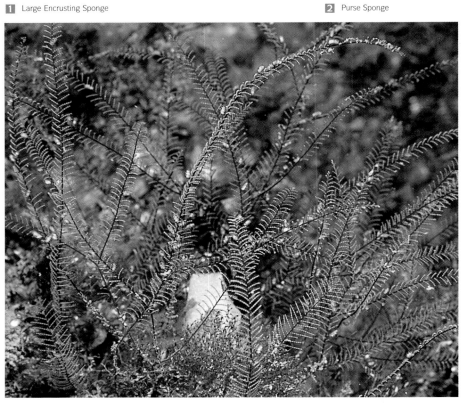

3 Sea Fern

1 SEA FIR

Eudendrium rameum

This is a short, stubby hydroid with a small, quite thick basal stem, quickly branching out. Each polyp head is arranged in alternate sequence, crowned with 24 tentacles. The male gnophores will also be clustered around the polyps. Found in fairly shallow water of less than 15m (50ft), the hydroid thicket will rarely exceed 20cm (8in).

2 SEA FEATHER

Gymnangium montagui

These rather striking fronds of *Gymnangium* stand over 10cm (4in) tall and occur in depths of over 20m (66ft), typically on exposed cliff walls where there is plenty of aeration and passing planktonic particles. Golden brown in colour, colonies may contain several hundred fronds.

JELLYFISH

Jellyfish are the free-floating medusa where the polyp stage of the life cycle has either been totally suppressed or extremely reduced. The upper surface of the jellyfish is generally smooth to touch and is known as the aboral or exumbrellar portion. The subumbrellar portion is underneath and contains the various combinations of tentacles and mouth parts which are armed with a variety of stinging cells. Jellyfish are quite capable of directional movement by pulsing the outer bell, creating a staccato propulsion. More often than not they are at the mercy of tidal movements and bad weather and can be washed up on tourist beaches in large numbers.

3 MOON JELLYFISH

Aurelia aurita

The Moon Jellyfish is one of the most common of all the jellyfish and occurs in all of our oceans and seas. Recognized by the four purplish or blue gonad rings found on the top of the bell, it can grow up to 40cm (1ft 4in) in diameter. The bell is surrounded by a ring of small tentacles and although not harmful to man, it preys on small fish and other planktonic larvae. This jellyfish uses the sun as a compass and forms breeding aggregations in late summer followed by extensive mutual migration into shallow coastal waters. The sedentary stage is found under rocky overhangs well aerated by tidal movement and releases young medusa into open waters in the spring.

4 CASSIOPEIA

Cothyloriza tubercolata

Occasionally called the 'Fried Egg Jellyfish', Cassiopeia comes into coastal waters in late summer driven by the need to spawn in shallow, well-lit waters. With a diameter of around 40cm (1ft 4in), this large, distinctive medusa has a creamy yellow bell top which is smaller than its tentacle ring. The tentacles are short and terminate in purple spots containing the stinging cells. Juvenile sand smelt and bogue are often found swimming within the 'protective' embrace of the tentacles.

5 LUMINESCENT JELLYFISH

Pelagia noctiluca

This oceanic jellyfish has a large, spotted bell of around 10cm (4in). These spots are actually warts armed with stinging cells. It has sixteen lobes, eight sense organs and eight marginal tentacles with four shorter frilled mouth tentacles under the bell. The marginal tentacles can extend over 1m (3ft 3in) long making them rather hazardous to swimmers during the summer months when this jellyfish can be quite prolific in inshore waters. There is no sessile stage in its reproduction, with the adult releasing juvenile medusae in the autumn.

6 BELL JELLYFISH

Rhizostoma pulmo

The largest of the jellyfish encountered in the Mediterranean, the outer bell can be over 1m (3ft 3in) in diameter. Very solid in construction, it overwinters in deeper water and migrates from the Atlantic. The eight short clubbed tentacles are subdivided into numerous frilled mouths and employ a mucus coating to trap food particles.

 Sea Fir *(above)*   Sea Feather *(right)*

3 Moon Jellyfish *(above)*   4 Cassiopeia *(below)*

5 Luminescent Jellyfish *(above)*

6 Bell Jellyfish *(left)*

SEA FANS or GORGONIANS

Sea fans are reasonably common throughout the Mediterranean and although there are few varieties, they are on the whole quite colourful, with the predominant species being *Paramuricea clavata* which can cover huge sections of cliff walls and wrecks. Owing to their sedentary nature, they prefer areas of moving water. Sea fans are characterized by an erect colony of individuals which form an intricate web of dividing branches with extended polyps. They are aligned along a single plane across the prevailing current with which to snare prey as it passes in the tidal stream.

1 PRECIOUS or RED CORAL
Corallium rubrum
Extensively collected and highly valued since classical times, Red Coral, although not growing in the traditional fan shape, is directly related to other gorgonians. The larger specimens have been intensively harvested over the years and are now only found in very deep water or in undiscovered caves. Each year, commercial coral divers are still killed or paralysed by the crippling 'bends' in their illegal search for greater and better-formed branches. Recognized as a protected species, the small, knobbly, three-dimensional branching colonies prefer deep caverns and other areas of very low light, including deep water. Most of the larger colonies have now all been fished out, leaving only tantalizing remnants of smaller colonies for us to still admire. The classic red colour is instantly recognizable with white widely spaced polyps. This fragile coral is variable in size depending on its location. In general diving areas in caves and caverns, it only grows to 3cm (1¼in); larger fans of this highly prized coral may be found in deeper waters.

2 YELLOW SEA FAN
Eunicella cavolinii
Very similar to *Eunicella verrucosa* except that the polyps are arranged in whorls at the tips of each branch. It enjoys vertical cliff walls where the fans, growing to around 40cm (1ft 4in) lie across the current to collect food particles. Found in shallow depths from 10 to 30m (33–100ft).

3 WHITE SEA FAN
Eunicella singularis
The most common of the sea fans and ranging throughout the Mediterranean, the White Sea Fan lives on rocks or wrecks alike in depths of over 12m (40ft) and can cover large areas. From a common stem, the branches are elongated and generally stretch upwards to a height of 30cm (12in). It has a microscopic, symbiotic algae, which may give it a slightly green coloration. The small polyps are darker than the body.

4 WARTY SEA FAN
Eunicella verrucosa
This species is closely related to *E. singularis*, but is more richly branched, forming a wider fan shape, more like a true gorgonian, up to 30cm (12in). Protruding out from the branches, the polyps are white in colour and have no pattern, arranged in double rows towards the tips. This distinctive species is found as far north as the British Isles and is always a delight for divers to find there, as the thought of exotic corals in British waters is something of a novelty! Preferring more sheltered locations and deeper water than *Eunicella singularis*, this species is preyed upon by various nudibranchs.

5 RED SEA FAN
Paramuricea clavata
The most common and colourful of all the Mediterranean sea fans, the Red Sea Fan adorns most vertical cliff faces in the central and western areas, growing up to 60cm (2ft). Depending on certain conditions, the fans will vary in colour from white through yellow to ruby red and purple, quite often on the same animal. Several areas are particularly well known for their extensive colonies, such as the Medas Islands, the Straits of Bonifacio between Corsica and Sardinia, the islands of Elba and Ustica, and the wrecks of Gibraltar. The Red Sea Fan particularly likes clear, clean water on offshore rocky seamounts where it gets the most benefit from coastal currents. The fans are also an important habitat for several species of nudibranch and mollusc, and even cat sharks lay their egg cases on them where the aerated water is most beneficial to the developing embryo (*see* p.89).

1 Precious Coral

2 Yellow Sea Fan

3 White Sea Fan

4 Warty Sea Fan

5 Red Sea Fan

1 GORGONIAN
Lophogorgia sarmentosa

Rosy red in colour, this sea fan has widely spaced branches which spread out from a common root stalk. The polyps are slightly lighter than the body colour and they create an effective net to capture food particles. Generally found in depths greater than 20m (66ft), this sea fan is quite rare in most areas.

OCTOCORALLIA

This family includes the soft corals, sea fans and sea pens. The medusoid stage in octocorallians has been suppressed and all of the animals represented in the Mediterranean are in fact colonies consisting of loosely connected polyps. The sea fans are more complex and create a hard skeleton underlying the polyps. Whilst this makes a perfect shape for netting passing food particles, sea fans are also prone to colonization by other species and can become completely overgrown. Sea pens tend to hide under soft sediments during the day and extend their soft bodies by infusing water and stretching upwards to feed at night.

2 SEA FINGERS
Alcyonium acaule

These hand-shaped colonies with stubby finger-like projections up to 12cm (5in) long are always rosy red in colour, with polyps which are tinged the same colour or even light yellow. This species can have quite a wide-spreading base attached to hard substrate. Closely related to all other Dead Men's Fingers, these compacted colonies can be found in depths of more than 20m (66ft), quite often on shipwrecks.

3 DEAD MEN'S FINGERS
Alcyonium palmatum

Compared with the previous one, this species forms more slender, upright branching colonies up to 12cm (5in) tall, connected to a hard substrata by a more slender columnar base. The body colour can vary from pale yellow through orange to red, but the polyps are always white and more spread out than on other related species. All of the *Alcyonium* species are characterized by their stubby, digiform-like ramifications, always cylindrical in shape and stretching from a common base, which has little or no polyps. They are heavily preyed upon by a number of different nudibranch species. The polyps tend only to extend for feeding during strong surge, current or at night; at other times, the 'fingers' resemble more the form of a jointed red sponge.

4 FALSE RED CORAL
Parerythropodium coralloides

This particular form of the family tends to form thin encrusting sheets which colonize gorgonian sea fans. Spreading up from the base, these colonial octocorallians have a ruby-red body and lighter, widely spaced, raised polyps. They are known to form small clumps on rocks and may even overgrow shells, but they are more commonly seen on *Eunicella* sea fans where the colour change is more striking.

5 ROUND SEA PEN
Veretillum cynomorium

Particularly common in the western Mediterranean around Morocco, Gibraltar and the Costa Del Sol, this species prefers soft, fine sand or a muddy substrate where its long foot can stay buried. If the habitat is threatened, perhaps in a violent storm or through pollution, it has the ability to release the water from its column, pull free of the seabed and gently roll off in the current until it finds another suitable habitat. Growing to over 20cm (8in) in length, the Round Sea Pen expands and retracts its cylindrical body by pumping water through its cavity. Usually only seen at night, this is one of the larger sea pens to be found in the Mediterranean. Pale orange or yellow in colour, the polyps are varied in colour from white to brown and can extend over 2cm (¾in).

6 COMMON SEA PEN
Virgularia mirabilis

Little seen, this small species up to 17cm (7in) in height prefers deeper waters with some current to spread its distinctly grouped polyps. Found in clusters of three to eight and located in two rows, the polyp and column are able to turn towards the prevailing current and create a net with which to catch food particles.

1 Gorgonian

2 Sea Fingers

3 Dead Men's Fingers

4 False Red Coral

5 Round Sea Pen

6 Common Sea Pen

HEXACORALLIA

This subdivision of the zoanthids is the largest family group and includes the anemones, zoanthids and corals. The name indicates that the polyp tentacles are arranged in groups of six rather than eight (octocorals such as Dead Men's Fingers or sea fans). Most anemones are solitary and attached to a hard substrate by means of a basal sucker. Others burrow into soft sand or mud creating a protective tube into which they can withdraw. Some species enjoy living in close proximity due to the very nature of their reproduction, such as the Snakelocks Anemone which multiplies by fission, creating two complete adults. Others produce live young. Some use pedal laceration where part of the column or base is detached and which grows into a new polyp. All anemones are carnivorous, trapping unwary small fish or invertebrates within the sticky grasp of their tentacles. Many creatures are also seemingly immune from the stinging cells and live within the range of the tentacles for protection from other predators. Two species of Hermit Crab are even more closely associated with anemones, playing direct host for additional protection.

1 ACTINOTHOE
Actinothoe sphryodeta
Most common around Gibraltar, Morocco and the eastern coast of southern Spain, this is a communal species found readily on shipwrecks and rocky surfaces. It has over a hundred tentacles, which are always white, with the disc ranging in colour from a fluorescent green to orange or brown and 4cm (1½in) across. It is able to fire sticky threads from the tentacles as a means of catching prey.

2 CLOAK ANEMONE
Adamsia carciniapados
A truly adaptive species, the Cloak Anemone wraps itself around the shell inhabited by the hermit crab *Pagarus prideaux*. The column of the anemone is pale fawn with garish magenta spots and the oral disc contains over five hundred small tentacles. The disc is usually found on the bottom of the crab's shell and enjoys the hermit crab's messy leftovers. Its size depends on the shell it covers. When threatened it secretes long, sticky, magenta threads.

3 TRUMPET ANEMONE
Aiptasia mutabilis
Living in holes or small crevices, the slender column (up to 17cm [7in] long) of this anemone is rarely seen. The column flares out widely and has about a hundred long, almost transparent tentacles. The tentacles do not retract readily; rather, they have additional protection in the form of a coiled sticky thread which shoots out from the tentacle tip if threatened. The anemone has a bluish tint due to the presence of zooxanthellae.

4 BERRIED ANEMONE
Alicia mirabilis
Sometimes referred to as the 'Wonder Anemone' owing to its amazing stretching ability, *Alicia* is better recognized by the numerous small berries which cover its body. These berries or tubercles are armed with stinging cells and can be quite harmful to human touch. During the day, it closes up and becomes a small inconspicuous lump only 10–15cm (4–6in) tall with its tentacles retracted. At night it can stretch over 1m (3ft 3in) and its long tentacles trap prey in the current.

5 SNAKELOCKS ANEMONE
Anemonia sulcata
One of the most common of the Mediterranean anemones, the Snakelocks Anemone is instantly recognizable by its 'gorgon-like' head of around two hundred tentacles, which are unable to be retracted as they are simply so numerous and so much larger than the body cavity. Generally grey or green in colour with purple-tipped tentacles, it is found on the lower shore where it is associated with a number of small crabs and gobies. It is up to 19cm (7½in) across.

6 HERMIT ANEMONE
Calliactis parasitica
Also living in association with a hermit crab, this large anemone, 5cm (2in) across, has quite a stiff column, cream in colour with vertical brown stripes. The oral parts are ringed by over seven hundred slender tentacles and the body is able to fire sticky threads or acontia when threatened. The hermit crab's shell can be found with large numbers of these heavy anemones, making it rather difficult for the crab to manoeuvre – but it is well protected!

1 Actinothoe

2 Cloak Anemone

3 Trumpet Anemone

4 Berried Anemone

5 Snakelocks Anemone

6 Hermit Anemone

1 DAISY ANEMONE

Cereus pedunculatus
Not as common as other anemones, this species lives happily amongst small stones, rocks or even a rough gravel seabed. In overall shades of brown, this anemone is tall and trumpet shaped with a wide oral disc surrounded by between five hundred and a thousand short tentacles. The column has some indistinct suckers to which it can attach bits of debris to create additional camouflage. It is 5cm (2in) across.

2 FIREWORKS ANEMONE

Cerianthus membranaceus
One of the largest of the Mediterranean species, *Cerianthus* prefers deep sheltered water or inside caverns, well away from strong sunlight. Secreting a parchment-like tube in the soft mud or sandy seabed, this anemone is distinguishable from other species by having two different types of tentacles. Inside the mouth are large numbers of small feeding tentacles, surrounded by very long, outer catching tentacles, which form an 'exploding firework' effect reaching over 1.50m (5ft). Sensitive to both pressure and light, this anemone is quite difficult to photograph as it is extremely retractile, being able to withdraw its tentacles in a split second.

3 GOLDEN ANEMONE

Condylactis aurantiaca
This large anemone lives in the soft sand in deep water, usually over 25m (80ft). The column is deep down in the sand, normally attached to a small stone. The oral disc is ringed with ninety-six fat tentacles with an overall diameter of around 20cm (8in). The anemone is sometimes mistaken for the Snakelocks Anemone due to the coloration of its tentacles, which are usually greenish in colour and tipped in purple. Large numbers of these are found around the wreck of the *Rozi* in Malta.

4 JEWEL ANEMONE

Corynactis viridis
Not usually associated with the Mediterranean, this tiny anemone is surprisingly common on off-shore sea mounts and vertical deep walls where it enjoys low sunlight and nutrient-rich water. With the polyps reaching only a maximum size of 10mm (½in), it is invariably still easy to spot owing to its iridescent bright colour. The short tentacles are characterized by having a knobbly tip. Able to reproduce asexually, many individuals of the same colour form are found together, often forming large sheets of colour.

5 DAHLIA ANEMONE

Cribinopsis crassa
Very similar to the *Urticina* species found in British waters, *Cribinopsis* is quite rare and only found on its own. Preferring a rocky crevice or hole in which to hide its body column, the short stubby tentacles are very retractile. Coming in various shades of blue and green owing to the presence of symbiotic zooxanthellae, it grows to around 12cm (4¾in) in diameter. This anemone is commonly associated with its symbiotic partner, the Amethyst Shrimp *Periclimenes amethysteus*.

ZOANTHIDS

Zoanthids are short colonial animals, very similar to anemones and other corals. The species have no skeleton and spread by means of an extending or creeping stolon. The single mouth of each polyp is ringed by two rows of tentacles containing a symbiotic alga known as zooxanthellae.

6 GOLDEN ZOANTHID

Parazoanthus axinellae
These are brilliant yellow- to orange-coloured polyps, which can grow as high as 2cm (¾in) and have twenty-four to thirty-six tentacles in two cycles. Preferring shaded areas, they are found under overhangs, at the entrances to caverns and are known to colonize many other types of more sedentary forms of marine life such as sea squirts, pen shells and even sea fans.

1 Daisy Anemone

2 Fireworks Anemone

3 Golden Anemone

4 Jewel Anemone

5 Dahlia Anemone

6 Golden Zoanthid

CORALS

The corals found in the Mediterranean are of the solitary polyp variety and although one may find large extensive colonies, the reef-building corals more commonly associated with tropical waters are not found owing to the lower temperature of the water. Unlike the anemones, corals are supported by a calcified skeleton, which can form large colonies.

1 STAR CORAL
Astroides calycularis
This brilliantly golden-coloured coral forms large sheets, which overgrow rocky surfaces. Reaching over 2cm (¾in) when fully extended, it forms large colonies. The calcified skeletons are connected by a common coenosteum with the mantle or bodies of the animals seemingly connected because they are packed so tightly together.

2 CUP CORAL
Caryophyllia smithii
One of the few coral polyps that inhabits British waters, the cup coral is particularly common in the western Mediterranean. This familiar species is recognized by its knobbly ended tentacles spreading out from a deeply grooved calcified disc approximately 1.5cm (½in) in diameter. As in all cup coral species, the tentacles are able to be retracted, allowing the calcified exterior to offer full protection to the animal.

3 MAT CORAL
Cladocora caespitosa
A migrant from the Atlantic, *Cladocora* is one of the few cup coral species that forms dense mats of individuals. Similar in structure to the reef-building corals of more tropical waters, this species has calcified 'heads' from 5 to 10mm (¼–½in) in diameter. Brownish-green in colour, the colonies can grow over 1m (3ft 3in) across.

4 YELLOW CUP CORAL
Leptosammia pruvoti
This solitary coral polyp is distinguishable by its brilliant, almost fluorescent, yellow colour. Quite tall, the stem or corallum can be 2cm (¾in) high. It prefers cave or cavern conditions as it is particularly light sensitive.

5 DARK SOLITARY CORAL
Phyllangia mouchezii
More notably found in the western Mediterranean, this is another species which has migrated into the Alboran Sea from the Atlantic. Solitary in disposition, it has a pronounced brown calcified corallum reaching over 2cm (¾in). The tentacles are almost transparent and knobbly.

BRYOZOANS

Bryozoans are delicate, sessile, colonial animals, containing many different families with equally many different characteristics. Bryozoans come into the category of false corals, as their general shape and structure often confuses many people into thinking that they are actually in the coral family.

6 LACE CORAL
Caberea boryi
Forming a delicate, creamy-white, lace basket, this small bryozoan has a calcified skeleton and grows to around 2.5cm (1in) in diameter. Found in depths of around 20 to 50m (66–165ft), it prefers a shaded location, but well aerated by water movement. It is commonly found in association with other species of bryozoan.

1   Star Coral

2   Cup Coral

3   Mat Coral

4   Yellow Cup Coral

5   Dark Solitary Coral

6   Lace Coral

1 FROND CORAL
Frondipora verrucosa
Very similar to *Caberea boryi* (*see* p.50) and often confused with this species, *Frondipora* has less of an obvious structure and does not form the basket-like shape. Rather, the fronds branch at different intervals and are thicker in structure. This species grows to a maximum size of 2.5cm (1in) and also enjoys fairly deep water.

2 FALSE CORAL
Myriapora truncata
The most common of all the species found in the central Mediterranean, False Coral inhabits deep water and the entrances to caves and caverns where it enjoys the low light conditions. Tinged rosy red and orange in colour, this distinctive bryozoan has widely spaced, short, rounded branches, which give the appearance of having been chopped off. Looking closely at the branches, you will notice minute pores. These contain the feeding parts of the organism, which are similar to coral polyps. Growing to a height of around 4cm (1½in), it is found in depths from 3m (10ft) to over 90m (300ft). Often confused with Antler Coral.

3 DEER HORN CORAL
Pentapora fascialis
Forming rounded clumps around 15cm (6in) in height, this delicate marine organism generally grows upright in poorly illuminated areas such as caverns. Tinged from amber to burnt orange in colour, the wide flattened branches divide and fuse together, overlapping to create a domed mass, similar to a coral head. Particularly delicate, it is easily dislodged by careless divers.

4 ENCRUSTING HYDROID
Schizomavella mamillata
Very hard and coral-like to the touch, this rarely seen encrusting species is tinged a salmon pink with raised creamy heads, which look like spots from a distance. Preferring low light areas, it is quite tolerant of poor water conditions and is known to encrust the keels of ships.

5 BRANCHING HORN WRACK
Securiflustra securifrons
Found in the North Sea, Atlantic and western Mediterranean, this pale creamy colonial bryozoan is stiff and calcified, but is not rigid like some of the other species, behaving more like a type of alga than a colony of animals. It can form quite dense clumps up to 10cm (4in) high, and it prefers a rocky substrate in well-aerated water.

6 NEPTUNE'S LACE
Sertella septentrionalis
Easily distinguished by its delicate, pinkish, lacy whorls, Neptune's Lace forms a cup-like shape with fluted edges. Over 5cm (2in) in height, it enjoys a cavern environment preferring low light conditions and is commonly associated with several other species of bryozoan, which enjoy the same habitat.

7 ANTLER CORAL
Smittina cervicornis
Antler Coral is often mistaken for *Myriapora* (False Coral) as they often intermingle on the same cliff wall. When using torch light, you can quickly see that not only is there a colour difference, but the size structure is also different. The colour of Antler Coral is pale cream and the branching segments are much more tightly packed together. It grows up to 10cm (4in) long.

1 Frond Coral

4 Encrusting Hydroid *(above)*

5 Branching Horn Wrack *(right)*

6 Neptune's Lace

2 False Coral *(above)*   **3** Deer Horn Coral *(below)*

7 Antler Coral

WORMS

There are many different species of worms to be found in the Mediterranean and the group is as diverse as it is interesting. There are the errant flat worms, free spirits to wander at will; there are the nemertid worms, which are unsegmented and have eyes and a mouth and are active hunters on the reef. The polychaete worms generally produce a parchment or calcified tube, which they can hide inside when not feeding. The bristle worms look like centipedes and are active predators on the reef; and there are the annelid worms, which burrow in soft sand and mud.

FLATWORMS

Flatworms have a leaf-like, flat body, which is able to undulate over the seabed by the aid of tiny cilia that beat rhythmically on their underside. Carnivorous animals, the mouth and anus are located on the underside and the head has two lobed projections, which form antenna. They are distinguishable from nudibranchs by their lack of gills.

1 PINK FLATWORM
Prostheceraeus giesbrechtii
This is the most commonly seen flatworm over the entire region, primarily due to its rather garish purple-and-white striped coloration. Growing to around 2cm (¾in) in length, it enjoys many different habitats from cave and cavern situations with little or no light to bright sandy conditions.

2 BROWN FLATWORM
Yungia aurantiaca
Also growing to around 2cm (¾in) in length, this flatworm has a golden- to light-brown body with a delicate white stripe around the outside of the body mantle or skirt. The body may also show a pattern of white spots over the entire length.

ANNELID WORMS

3 GREEN TONGUE
Bonellia viridis
This small exclusive species is instantly recognizable by its long, green, tongue-like proboscis, which splits into two at the end. Gently lobed, it is able to extend its proboscis over 80cm (2ft 8in) from its hold fast under stones or from a rocky crevice. All *Bonellia* are female and are well known for being able to determine the sex of their larvae. If the drifting larvae, which land on the large proboscis, are male, they cling to the

body and change into dwarf males, which then enter the intestines and sexual organs of the female. If the larvae are female they do not attach themselves but will settle onto a suitable habitat and develop into females within a year.

POLYCHAETE WORMS

Polychaete worms are segmented worms with eyes and are more commonly recognized as the wreathy tuft of bristles or fans, which protrude from a tube. Split into two families: the errant worms, which wander at will; and the sedentary worms, which are attached.

ERRANT WORMS

4 SEA MOUSE
Aphrodita aculeata
Around 10cm (4in) long, the sea mouse has an elongated oval body covered in fine, grey hairs. The flanks are the most distinctive, having iridescent green and golden hairs or bristles and lustrous brown spines. An active hunter on soft sand or mud, it is able to burrow into the substrate.

5 BEARDED FIRE WORM
Hermodice carunculata
This species is found in all of the world's tropical and subtropical waters, being equally as common in the Caribbean as it is in the Mediterranean. It is able to grow up to 30cm (12in) and is an active predator on the reef. It is characterized by the pale brown to gold or red iridescent, slender, segmented body with a series of tufts of white bristle hairs on its flanks. If accidentally rubbed against the skin, the hairs are needle sharp and easily penetrate the skin, causing severe irritation not unlike a bad burn. It attacks corals and hydroids and is known to kill and eat small sea urchins.

1 Pink Flatworm

2 Brown Flatworm

3 Green Tongue

4 Sea Mouse

5 Bearded Fire Worm

SEDENTARY WORMS

1 DELICATE CORAL WORM
Filograna implexa
Filograna is one of the most delicate of all the tube worm species. Growing in large interlacing colonies over 15cm (6in) in diameter, its protective tubes are calcareous and only 1–2mm (ca. ⅟₁₆in) in diameter. Often growing attached to fan corals, the crown or fan tuft is only 5mm (¼in) across and its base is pale yellow or orange, giving a spotted appearance to the colony. Extremely fragile, the tubes are very vulnerable to damage.

2 MUD WORM
Myxicola infundibulum
Quite distinctive in appearance, *Myxicola* enjoys a muddy or soft sand substrate, quite often at the entrance to caverns where there is a continuous collection of detritus. Surprisingly versatile, this species of sedentary worm has been observed by the author around the British Isles, Scandinavia and even off Newfoundland, where it enjoys an interesting habitat on several deep wrecks at temperatures plunging to 0°C. Usually pale purple or greyish-white in colour, the protruding fan is crater-like in appearance and is quickly retracted should danger threaten. Each of the tips of the fan is a dark brown and the fan tentacles are connected by a thin film. The parchment-like tube is rectangular and rarely protrudes above ground level. The worm is 3cm (1¼in) long.

3 INQUISITIVE TUBE WORM
Polycirrus sp.
Often overlooked by divers, this small worm is easily recognized by its trail of numerous thread-like tentacles, which snake over the rocky surface searching for food particles in the surrounding area. The main body of the worm is always hidden inside a hole or rocky crevice and is quite often additionally protected by sponge growth. The white tentacles can be over 15cm (6in) long.

4 SMALL TUBE WORM
Pomatocerous triqueter
Often overlooked due to its small size, this tiny tube worm is quite common on the lower shore and can be found on many stones and rocky surfaces. Characterized by having an obvious diamond-shaped tube, often overgrown by algae, the mouth of the tube can be tinged from green to red. The spiral fan tuft is spotted and can be virtually any colour, from white and blue to green and purple. The raised calcareous tubes are usually curled and around 5cm (2in) long.

5 WHITE TUFTED WORM
Protula tubularia
Often mistaken for *Serpula vermicularis*, this species is generally larger with the fan tuft being around 3cm (1¼in) in diameter. It is generally white or pale cream in colour and will have regular spots up each of the tentacles. Spirally extended, this animal is also differentiated by not having a protective operculum or trap door for its calcified tube.

6 PEACOCK WORM
Sabella pavonina
A common species, generally inhabiting soft sand or muddy sea floors in sheltered low-light conditions. The tube is of parchment construction and is quite stiff. The head of the fan is around 7cm (2¾in) in diameter and is coloured in shades of brown or orange in concentric rings, giving a very pleasant effect when viewed. It is more regularly associated with the cliffs and wrecks of the Scottish west coast and the fjords of Scandinavia, where this tube worm can form large colonies in deep colder waters with poor light. Light and pressure sensitive, the fans are quickly retracted inside its tube should danger threaten. It would appear that the Peacock Worm is equally at home in strong current or sheltered deep inside caverns, as it is in the Mediterranean.

1 Delicate Coral Worm

2 Mud Worm

3 Inquisitive Tube Worm

4 Small Tube Worm

5 White Tufted Worm

6 Peacock Worm

1 VARIABLE TUBE WORM
Serpula vermicularis
This species is very distinctive in colour, ranging from brilliant orange to purple. It is only 2cm (¾in) in diameter and slightly horseshoe-shaped. The protective cap or operculum of its calcified tube home is clearly visible. Enjoying rocky walls and low light in well-aerated water, this tube worm is light- and pressure-sensitive and can quickly retract its feeding fan should danger approach. Often mistaken for *Protula tubularia* (*see* p.56).

2 SPIRAL TUBE WORM
Spirographis spallanzani
This is the largest of the tube worms and grows out on long thin parchment tubes perhaps 30cm (12in) long. It enjoys a mixed habitat of cave and cavern, rock wall or Posidonia beds. Spirograph shaped, the fan may consist of eight or ten whorls, which are varicoloured. They are light- and pressure-sensitive and often withdraw back into their tubes before you can get near them. The fan may be as much as 15cm (6in) in diameter.

MOLLUSCS
Phylum Mollusca

The molluscs form the largest and most diverse group of marine animals on the planet and probably the most familiar group of invertebrates. The family includes nudibranchs or sea slugs, chitons, snails, bivalves, octopus and squid. There are some 75,000 species in eight different families found in the world's oceans. Most of the species have common characteristics such as an external shell, a soft body with a muscular foot and a rasping, tongue-like radula for feeding, with gills of some kind for respiration. All lay eggs and of the eight groups, three are fairly common around these shores.

CEPHALOPODS

The cephalopods are by far the most successful of the Mollusca and octopus are common throughout the Mediterranean. Extremely intelligent and adaptable, they are free-swimming, fast-moving predators with well-developed eyes and sensory systems. All of the cephalopods are able to change their shape and coloration to suit their environment or to exhibit and display to a mate or a would-be predator. They are also considered prized catches and feature in most coastal seafood restaurants!

3 MUSKY OCTOPUS
Eledone moschata
Usually mistaken for the Common Octopus, this species is fairly common in shallow waters around the western Mediterranean. With a body length of 15cm (6in) and arms to around 40cm (1ft 4in), it is predominantly brown in colour with darker brown spots arranged irregularly over the body and webs. The animal is distinguished by the single row of suckers. The common name comes from the musky smell it exudes when taken out of the water. The female of the species lays around five hundred eggs about 10mm (½in) long.

4 WHITE-SPOTTED OCTOPUS
Octopus macropus
The White-spotted Octopus is more commonly seen at night when it is an active hunter. It appears to be exclusively nocturnal and there are virtually no records of the species being seen during the day. The body grows to around 15cm (6in) and the arms are over 1m (3ft 3in) long. It is recognized by the pairs of white spots down the long arms and an overall reddish-brown body.

1 Variable Tube Worm
(top left)

2 Spiral Tube Worm
(top right)

3 Musky Octopus
(left)

4 White-spotted Octopus
(below)

1 COMMON OCTOPUS
Octopus vulgaris
Common indeed, this species of octopus is very wide ranging and is found and commercially fished all round the Mediterranean. Over 20,000 tonnes are taken annually off the North African coast alone. With a total body length of around 1m (3ft 3in) and maximum arm spread of 3m (10ft) in diameter, the body is stout and warty in appearance with two rows of suckers found on the arms. The animal preys on crabs and lobster, and will also eat shellfish. The den of the octopus is usually discovered by the amount of shell debris found outside its lair.

2 COMMON CUTTLEFISH
Sepia officinalis
This species grows to over 45cm (1½ft) long and has an internal cuttlebone, which is a chambered, gas-filled shell used for buoyancy control. Possessing eight arms and two longer feeding tentacles, adults of the species are recognized by the white bands across the bodies and small white spots on the upper surface of the fins. The arms have four rows of suckers and it actively stalks its prey around Posidonia beds and inshore reefs. Like all species, it is characterized by its ability to change colour and body texture at will.

3 CALAMARI SQUID
Loligo vulgaris
Growing to over 75cm (2½ft) long, this is the most common squid found in the Mediterranean. The species inhabits the water column to all depths, but comes into shallow coastal waters to spawn. The female lays around 20,000 eggs in pale white or grey gelatinous strings attached to the sea floor or hard objects. This squid is caught commercially by a variety of trawl nets and with night lights and jigs.

GASTROPODS

Gastropods form the largest class of the Mollusca family and the body form is widely varied. It includes all univalved shellfish such as limpets, periwinkles and snails. They usually have a shell of one piece and live mostly on the shore or sea bottom. This group also includes the opisthobranchs, which have no shell at all.

4 CHITON
Chiton olivaceus
This ancient species of animal is particularly distinctive by its eight hinged overlapping plates, which allow the animal to fold itself up. Oval shaped and tinged with various shades of green, it is able to clamp onto rocks with the aid of a strong muscular foot. Common on the shoreline and surf zone, it enjoys aerated water and grows to a maximum size of around 5cm (2in).

5 QUEEN SCALLOP
Aequipecten opercularis
This small scallop is highly prized in the fish market and is commercially harvested throughout the Mediterranean and Atlantic. It grows to around 9cm (3½in) in diameter and has twenty, sculpted, bold ridges on each side. It lives on mud and soft, sandy seabeds. *Ecology*: The species usually gets overgrown by a variety of sponges and it is extremely mobile when danger threatens. With the aid of its muscular joint, it opens and closes the two halves of the shell rapidly, thus providing a jet-propelled escape.

6 WHELK
Buccinulum corneum
This gastropod mollusc has a thick, spindle-shaped shell with an oval opening and an upturned tip where its eye stalks protrude. Usually pink and beige in colour, it grows to around 6cm (2½in) and enjoys grazing amongst Posidonia and algae-encrusted rock surfaces.

7 MEDITERRANEAN CERITH
Cerithium vulgatum
This tower shell grows to 6.5cm (2½in) and has a thick and broad sculpture with prominent ridges at the growth lines. It has quite a large aperture and thick, flared lips. It is common in soft sand and shell debris areas where it filter feeds. *Ecology*: This species is a common home for Hermit Crabs and you can often see large numbers of them together on a dead fish or crab.

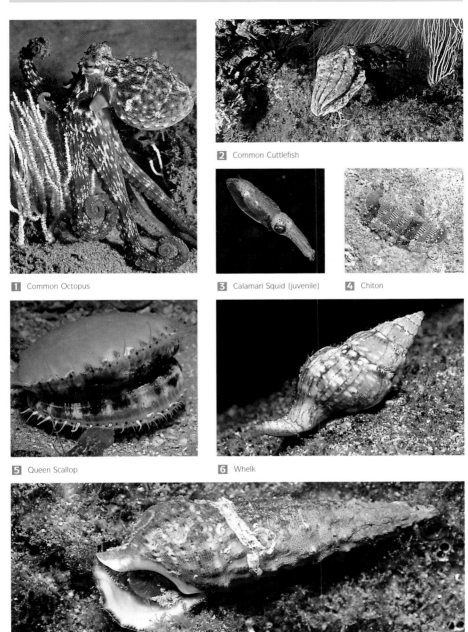

1 Common Octopus

2 Common Cuttlefish

3 Calamari Squid (juvenile)

4 Chiton

5 Queen Scallop

6 Whelk

7 Mediterranean Cerith

1 TRITON TRUMPET
Charonia tritonis
The largest of the trumpet shells and quite rare in the Mediterranean, it feeds on starfish and is an active predator. It can grow over 40cm (1ft 4in) and is constructed of irregular spires, often overgrown by calcareous algae. The foot is beige-spotted with brown, and the eye stalks have two dark bands.

2 MEDITERRANEAN CONE SHELL
Conus mediterraneus
Distinctively shaped, this cone shell can grow to 7cm (2¾in). The shell is typically broadest at the abapical end of the slit-like aperture, which tapers towards the open siphon canal. It has a short spire with only three or four whorls and the entire shell is smooth and shiny with mottled brown striations.

3 MEDITERRANEAN COWRIE
Cyprea lurida
Fairly common on night dives, this species of cowrie grows to around 3cm (1¼in) and is found in central and eastern areas of the Mediterranean. It has brownish, broad bands across its back and at both ends. The mantle of the animal is also brown with spiky protuberances and when fully extended is difficult to spot.

4 SPOTTED COWRIE
Cyprea spurca
This colourful cowrie is relatively rare as it is a night-time predator, preferring to hide well away in a rocky crevice during the day. More likely to be found in a cave situation, this cowrie is tinged orange and rusty brown and eats various types of sponge and bryozoan. The shell is kept smooth and shiny by the animal's mantle skirt, which completely covers the shell whilst moving.

5 ABALONE
Haliotis lamellosa
Confined to the Mediterranean, the abalone shell grows to 7cm (2¾in) and enjoys a shaded position, more often than not hiding under rocks during the day. It is recognized by its low spire and limpet shape, and the outer surface has a keel of small round holes. The fleshy foot is not only able to attach itself firmly to a rock, it also allows for easy propulsion. The species feeds on red algae. The inside of the shell is of iridescent mother of pearl.

6 TUBE SNAIL
Lementina arenoria
This is a curious mollusc of a diverse family with nine species in total to be found, which are easily confused with each other. Resembling a tube worm, the Tube Snail has a wide obvious shell and can grow up to approximately 1.5cm (½in) in diameter, often overgrown with algae and small corals. The animal has no operculum and the mouth of the tube shows the reddish-brown snail streaked with a golden-yellow pattern. It lives inside this tube all the time and fishes for prey by extending a mucous net, capturing plankton and transporting it to the gut by ciliary currents produced by its gills.

7 SPINY FILE SHELL
Lima lima
This file clam always lives in a rocky crevice and is usually seen when it extends its white, sticky feeding tentacles from the mouth of the shell. With a shell of equal halves, it soon grows large enough to be unable to move from its home and will eventually die in the some location. Those found in the open are able to swim in the same way as a scallop does, by expanding and contracting a strong muscle, opening and closing the shell rapidly, providing propulsion.

1 Triton Trumpet

2 Mediterranean Cone Shell *(above)*

3 Mediterranean Cowrie *(left)*

4 Spotted Cowrie

5 Abalone

6 Tube Snail

7 Spiny File Shell

1 COMMON MUSSEL
Mytilus edulis

Located extensively in shallow water, particularly around the surf zone, mussels are a highly prized addition to the Mediterranean seafood diet. Commercially farmed in a number of areas, wild mussels are coloured a dark bluish-purple and are able to attach themselves together in large groups by means of a renewable byssus or stiff secreted thread. They grow up to 5cm (2in) long and there are some 36 species found in European seas.

2 GOLDEN CARPET SHELL
Paphia aurea

This small bivalve is found in large numbers in rough sand and shell gravel and is harvested mercilessly. Growing to 3cm (1¼in) across and roughly triangular in shape, the concentric sculpture has obvious growth rings and is overlaid with an intricate zig-zag pattern.

3 NOBLE PEN SHELL
Pinna nobilis

Resembling a partly folded fan, these giant mussels are highly sought after as souvenirs and are a protected species in the Mediterranean. In special circumstances, the shell can attain a height of over 1m (3¼ft). It prefers to live amongst Posidonia. The outer shell is quite rough and makes an ideal home for many different species of algae and sponge and it also harbours a few commensal crabs and shrimps within its body cavity. In the 19th century, the byssus threads were collected, dried and then woven into gloves, shawls and stockings, similar in texture to silk. These products were greatly sought after by the upper classes.

4 ROUGH PEN SHELL
Pinna rudis

Much smaller than its cousin, this pen shell grows to around 10cm (4in) across and has a much flatter anterior lip. This fan mussel prefers very low light conditions and a hard rocky substrate where it grows from a crevice. Also found on rough gravel sea floors at the entrance to caverns, this rare species has delicate raised whorls along the outside of the almost translucent shell.

5 SMOOTH CARPET SHELL
Pitar rudis

Extensively collected for public consumption, the Smooth Carpet Shell, up to 2½cm (1in) long, has a shiny outer surface coloured in shades of beige and golden brown with darker concentric circles of colour. It prefers a soft sand or muddy seabed, where this species can occur in vast numbers.

6 WINGED OYSTER
Pteria hirundo

This very distinctive oyster has equal valves to the shell and is usually found attached to gorgonian sea fans, where it enjoys the strong current to filter-feed passing plankton. Utilizing byssus threads to attach itself to the sea fan, this shell grows to 6cm (2⅜in) in diameter, vaguely oval in overall shape but with a distinct thin ear or wing.

7 ROCK SCALLOP
Spondylus spp.

This species is probably *Spondylus gaederopus*, but as always with these bivalves it is difficult to identify owing to the covering of distinctive raised spines on the shell covered by the sponge *Crambe crambe*. The bottom half of the shell is firmly adhered to the rocky surface and reaches 12cm (5in) in length. Preferring caves and low light conditions, this scallop has its distinctive double row of eyes around the body cavity and pale-cream inner muscle. Highly prized both for its meat and pearl producing capabilities, the species is in decline throughout the Mediterranean.

1 Common Mussel

2 Golden Carpet Shell

3 Noble Pen Shell

4 Rough Pen Shell

5 Smooth Carpet Shell *(above left)*

6 Winged Oyster *(above)*

7 Rock Scallop *(left)*

1 TRUNCATED WHELK
Truncculariopis trunculus
Growing to around 8.5cm (3½in), this whelk has a very rough exterior shell. It grazes on various algae and, although it is often seen singularly, it can form large breeding groups and is known to mass spawn. With only a few concentric whorls of the shell, the anterior is markedly upturned and protects the eye stalks.

2 WARTY VENUS
Venus verrucosa
This is a stout bivalve with a shell of equal halves formed of more than twenty concentric growth rings. Growing to around 6cm (2½in) in diameter, it is yellowish-white or orange in colour and lives partly buried in rough sand and shell gravel. This species is highly prized by octopus, which often use the shells to seal the entrance to their den.

SEA HARES

Herbivorous sea hares are characterized by rather fleshy bodies, which are swollen towards the rear and a head, which is split into pairs of lobed oral and sensory tentacles. Sea hares have the ability to release clouds of purplish ink as well as milky white, sticky threads as a means of defence.

3 GIANT SEA HARE
Aplysia fasciata
Growing to over 40cm (1ft 4in) and with a weight of nearly 2kg (4½lb), the Giant Sea Hare is a dark peaty brown in colour with a mauve tinged edge to the skirt. It feeds on a large variety of seaweeds and is usually found in pairs.

4 SMALL SEA HARE
Aplysia punctata
Growing to only 20cm (8in), half the size of its cousin, the Small Sea Hare is also a much lighter brown in colour, although this colour varies depending on the diet. It is delicately marked with lighter spots over a mottled or blotched body.

PLEUROBRANCHS

Pleurobranchs still have the vestiges of a shell, which may be either internal or external. They have acid-secreting glands for defence and most species are carnivorous.

5 UMBRELLA SNAIL
Umbraculum mediterraneum
This is a very distinctive oval slug, 4cm (1½in) long. It looks as though it is carrying an algae-covered limpet as a hat and owing to the hundreds of lobed portions to the body, is sometimes mistaken for a shell with its egg cases. It has two short rhinophores, or sensory tentacles, at the head and enjoys light and well-aerated water.

NUDIBRANCHS

The name 'nudibranch' quite literally means 'naked gills' and these are snails, which have lost their shells. This is the largest order of Opisthobranchs and the body of the various species varies widely, but they also have similar characteristics in that they usually have obvious rhinophores at the head and a set of gills at the rear of the body. They may have various projections dotted about and all are carnivorous.

6 WHITE-TIPPED NUDIBRANCH
Coryphella pedata
This species grows up to 5cm (2in) long and has seven paired clusters of cerata, all of which are white tipped. The body is a uniform purple and may have some light spots along its back. It feeds on various hydroids including *Eudendrium*. Not to be confused with Purple Nudibranch.

7 MIGRATING AEOLID
Cratena peregrina
This species is quite common in central and northern regions, where it can occur in quite large numbers, depending on the time of year. It has six clusters of cerata merging to brown with a purple tip. The oral tentacles are tinged in blue to white and there is a distinct orange flash on the head between the rhinophores. It grows up to 5cm (2in) long.

1 Truncated Whelk *(top left)*

2 Warty Venus *(above)*

3 Giant Sea Hare *(left)*

4 Small Sea Hare *(below left)*

5 Umbrella Snail *(below)*

6 White-tipped Nudibranch

7 Migrating Aeolid

1 SEA LEMON
Dendrodoris limbata
Typically oval in shape and lemon to brown in colour, it has a blotched body with a yellow frill. This species is quite small, only growing to 2.5cm (1in) and inhabits deeper water where it feeds on a variety of hydroids, bryozoans and even sponges.

2 WHITE LINED DORID
Doriopsilla pelseneri
Another distinct species, this dorid is a golden yellow in colour and grows to 3cm (1¼in) long. Oval in shape, the body is covered in a tracery of fine white lines. Both the rhinophores and gills are the same colour as the body and are retractile.

3 ELYSIA
Elysia viridis
This colourful and delicate opisthobranch grows to around 2.5cm (1in) in length and has rudimentary eyes situated behind the rhinophores. It tends to be shades of green in colour owing to the absorption of the chloroplasts from the algae that it eats. This common species has been observed laying eggs and eating the invasive *Caulerpa racemosa*.

4 PURPLE NUDIBRANCH
Flabellina affinis
The Purple Nudibranch is different from *Coryphella pedata* (*see* p.66) in that it does not have the white tips to its cerata. A garish violet colour, it is also deeply tinged with red and lives on the polyps of hydrozoa. Growing up to 5cm (2in) long, it has six to nine paired clusters of cerata and its rhinophores are also the same as the body colour. It feeds on species of the hydroid *Eudendrium*.

5 LADY GODIVA
Godiva banyulensis
Quite common throughout the region, this aeolid has a beige body with distinct white lines down each side of its back and outside of the skirt. The oral tentacles are tinged with blue and the seven clusters of cerata along the back are tinged with fawn and brown with a golden tip. It grows up to 5cm (2in) long.

6 ELEGANT SEA SLUG
Hypselodoris elegans
This is one of the largest nudibranchs to be found in the Mediterranean, growing to over 15cm (6in), and it comes in a variety of body colours, all of which are rather bright and garish. Ranging from brilliant yellow to violet and even green, the gill tuft is very prominent, almost like a flower. The body mass has a frilly edge and the species enjoys fairly deep water, feeding on encrusting hydroids and coral polyps. There would appear to be some confusion over this species of *Hypselodoris* as it is known by various other names, depending on the colour pattern. Scientists are still not convinced that these other colour forms are separate subspecies, rather than just colour changes due to the different diets from various areas of the Mediterranean. Names that you will come across in various regional guide books are *H. picta*, *H. webbi* and *H. valenciennesi*, but it is generally assumed that they are all the same species.

7 TRI-COLOUR DORIS
Hypselodoris tricolor
Much smaller in size, this species grows to only 2cm (¾in) and is a brilliant blue in colour with equal horizontal yellow lines and another yellow line completely encircling the body. The rhinophores are dark blue, as are the gills.

8 CRYSTAL TIPS
Janolus cristatus
This species has an oval, flattened shape and is fringed all round the 7.5cm (3in) body by golden cerata or tentacles, each tipped with white and iridescent blue. The rhinophores are white and non-retractile. This species feeds on bryozoans. Widely distributed throughout the Mediterranean, Canary Islands, Bay of Biscay and the British Isles, it is an active night-time predator. Crystal Tips can be found on many different substrates, preferring clean, shallow and sheltered waters. It is more often than not seen wandering over the sandy seabed in search of another meal.

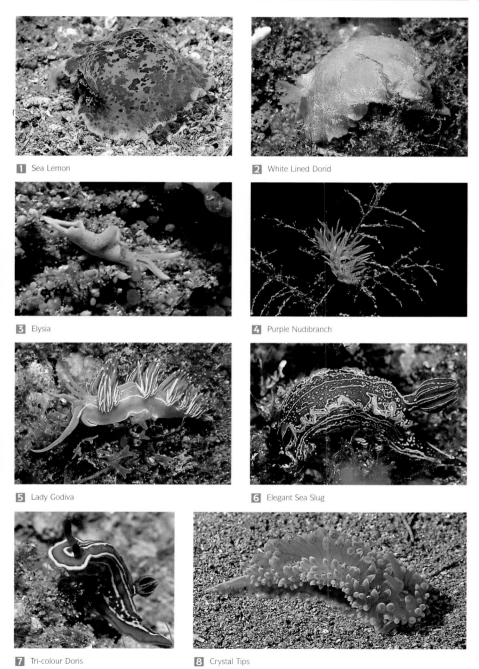

1 Sea Lemon

2 White Lined Dorid

3 Elysia

4 Purple Nudibranch

5 Lady Godiva

6 Elegant Sea Slug

7 Tri-colour Doris

8 Crystal Tips

1 SPOTTED DORIS
Discodoris atromaculata
Particularly distinctive in appearance, with a light-coloured body and dark brown, irregular spots; usually growing to around 12cm (4¾in) in length, it is often quite smaller. The eight gills and rhinophores are both white. This species feeds almost exclusively on the sponge *Petrosia ficiformis* and can be found in open, well-lit areas as well as deep caverns and caves.

2 LEATHERY DORIS
Platydoris argo
Burnt orange or brown in colour and roughly oval in shape, the outer skirt of the body is deeply ruffled, giving it a rather indistinct outline. This curious doris is always found in association with a partner or partners, usually moving along in pairs, just slightly overlapping. It can grow to 10cm (4in) long and its rhinophores and gills are deeply set back from its frame and are totally retractile.

3 FOUR-LINED NUDIBRANCH
Polycera quadrilineata
A common sea slug in the western Mediterranean, this species is an Atlantic immigrant and is common throughout the Bay of Biscay and up to Scandinavia. It has a distinct white body with yellow stripes around the frame but may have lots of black spots and lines and has four prominent yellow-tipped oral tentacles. It grows to 3.5cm (1⅜in) and feeds on a variety of bryozoans and hydroids.

4 CEUTA SEA SLUG
Tambja ceuta
Largely confined to the Straits of Gibraltar and the Moroccan coast, this species is a dull greyish-green or blue in colour with darker blue or violet lines and pale yellow along the body. It grows to over 4cm (1⅜in) long.

CRUSTACEANS
Phylum Crustacea

This large phylum has over 30,000 members worldwide and crustaceans can be found in every marine habitat. In general they have segmented bodies with a head, thorax and abdomen and are heavily protected by calcareous outer body armour. Most divers see the obvious decapod species, which have ten legs, which, depending on the species, are adapted for walking, feeding, swimming, defence, food capture, respiration and even the carrying of eggs.

SEA SPIDER

5 SEA SPIDER
Nymphon gracile
This sea spider is regarded as very rare, principally due to it being quite small and difficult to find at only 10–15mm (ca. ⅝in) long. The body is smooth and pale cream to light brown in colour, and is rigidly segmented. The legs are of equal length and may well have bits of detritus attached to them. Widely distributed, it is commonly found at the base of sea fans and around hydroids and various calcareous algae, where it is able to hide its vulnerable body should danger threaten.

BARNACLES

6 STAR BARNACLE
Chthalamus stellatus
Newly developed barnacles, whilst in the plankton, display their feeding arm. It looks like a catching mitt, which is what it is. A distant relation of the crabs, barnacles settle onto a suitable habitat in the shallow water surf zone where they develop a protective shell of calcified rigid overlapping plates. Only a few millimetres across, they are packed closely together. They are able to seal themselves off in bad conditions or exceptionally low tides and are able to live for a short while out of the water.

1 Spotted Doris

2 Leathery Doris

3 Four-lined Nudibranch

4 Ceuta Sea Slug

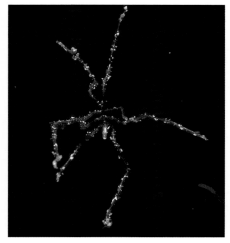

5 Sea Spider

6 Star Barnacle

1 GOOSE BARNACLE

Lepas anserifera

The Goose Barnacle adopts a similar procedure in catching prey to that of the Star Barnacle, but although this species is also sedentary in nature, it attaches itself onto floating bits of debris, ships' keels and piers. Tolerant of poor water conditions, the Goose Barnacle is around 4cm (1½in) long and has a long, leathery foot and a strong, calcified, protective head where the catching mitt is kept.

SHRIMPS

2 OPOSSUM SHRIMP

Paramysis helleri

Found throughout the Mediterranean and Black Sea, the Opossum Shrimp occurs in large numbers and is an important food source for small fish. Growing to only 1.1cm (ca. ½in) in length, it lives close to the sea floor or rocky crevices where it can quickly hide from predators. Vast numbers of Opossum Shrimps can be found in the cave systems along the coast of northern Spain, the Balearics, Corsica and Sardinia during the summer months. Deep inside the caves, they are preyed upon by slipper lobsters, Unicorn Shrimps, Common Shrimps and even Anthias, which will venture away from the light of day after this veritable feast.

3 ELEGANT SHRIMP

Palaemon elegans

This is one of the more common shrimps found around the coastline and is normally associated with a rocky subsurface. Quite a stout prawn, growing to around 6cm (2½in), it has strong, dark reddish-brown stripes on a fairly transparent body. Generally found in association with Dead Men's Fingers and preferring low light conditions, this shrimp is an active forager by dusk and at night time. It is an important food source and is harvested commercially in a number of Mediterranean countries that have vast sand banks and shallow sheltered bays, such as the north African coast.

4 COMMON SHRIMP

Palaemon serratus

Unlike the Elegant Shrimp, this species prefers low light and even pitch black conditions and is more commonly found deep inside caves. The species is also much larger at 11cm (4½in). Although this species of shrimp enjoys a communal lifestyle with large numbers of its own species or alongside Unicorn Shrimps, more often than not it is found on its own, wandering around deeper caverns in search of Opossum Shrimps or edible detritus.

5 AMETHYST SHRIMP

Periclimenes amethysteus

One of the most colourful of all the Mediterranean shrimps, the Amethyst Shrimp has a symbiotic relationship with a few anemones, but principally *Cribinopsis crassa*. Stout of body, up to 2.5cm (1in) long and nearly transparent, it has pinkish, well-defined markings with long, beige pincers and blue-striped legs. Seemingly rather docile when near its anemone protection, it is able to dodge very rapidly out of the way should danger threaten. The species can also be found around Posidonia seagrass beds, where its bright colours are a very rare delight for divers.

6 UNICORN SHRIMP

Plesionica narval

More common in the central and western Mediterranean, the Unicorn Shrimp is found deep in caverns and at night. It has a distinctive clear body with red and gold lateral lines and quite often blue eggs attached to the underside, and can grow to 10cm (4in). Like many other shrimp species, it starts life as a male and changes to female with maturity.

7 CLEANER SHRIMP

Stenopus spinosus

The Mediterranean Cleaner Shrimp is very timid and only rarely seen, and then only at dusk or during the night. It is a golden orange or rust brown in colour with long, white feelers with which it communicates with the various fish species that it cleans of parasites. Performing an important role in the health of the reef, this small shrimp is closely related to the Banded Coral Shrimp of more tropical waters. It is 10cm (4in) long.

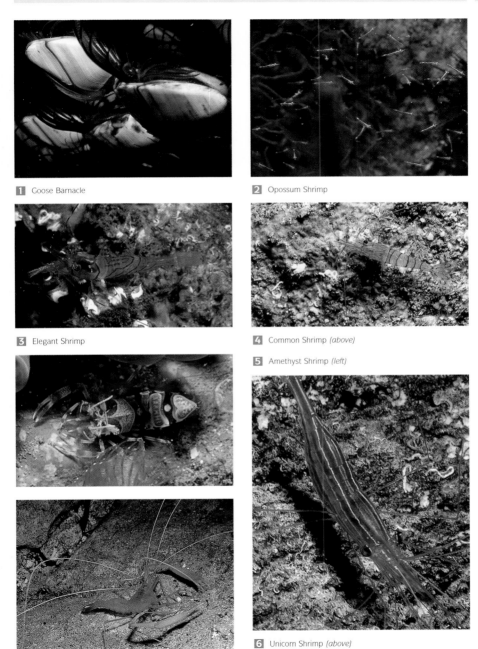

1 Goose Barnacle

2 Opossum Shrimp

3 Elegant Shrimp

4 Common Shrimp *(above)*

5 Amethyst Shrimp *(left)*

6 Unicorn Shrimp *(above)*

7 Cleaner Shrimp *(left)*

LOBSTERS

1 STRIDENT SQUAT LOBSTER
Galathea strigosa
There are a few species of squat lobster in these waters and they are migrants from the Atlantic. Principally found in the western Mediterranean, they have become quite adaptable to warmer waters. The most colourful of all is the Strident Squat Lobster with its brilliant orange-red body armour and vibrant, iridescent blue stripes across its head and around the eyes. It grows up to a maximum length of around 10cm (4in) and prefers low-light shaded conditions.

2 LONG-CLAWED SQUAT LOBSTER
Munida rugosa
Often referred to as 'Langoustine' by the French, the Long-clawed Squat Lobster enjoys a deep-water habitat where it lives under stones and rocks. Often associated with brittle starfish beds and ascidians. Instantly recognized by its bright orange, fairly slim body, which is around 30cm (12in) long and its chelipeds or pincer arms at twice the body length.

3 SMALL LOCUST LOBSTER
Scyllaris arctus
Extremely light sensitive, this very shy, small slipper lobster lives in deep caves with very little light. Growing to only 12cm (4¾in) in length, it has plate-like antennae, which have rounded, lobed edges. It is a mottled brown in colour with splashes of red in the joints of the abdomen and a red ring around the slightly stalked eye. It has a very broad tail to allow for rapid movement and its eight obvious striped legs are used to grip onto the undersides of cavern ceilings and walls. When approached, it literally hops in reverse very quickly out of danger. It lives in fairly large colonies and is a sociable lobster.

4 COMMON LOBSTER
Homarus gammarus
This lobster is more associated with Atlantic and North Sea waters, but it is surprising to note that it is quite common in the Mediterranean. Preferring to live under large boulders or in deep rocky crevices, the Common Lobster is a nocturnal feeder and divers are more likely to see it at night. It is a large, robust animal, bluish in colour with stout pincers, one of which is modified for gripping, the other modified for cutting. Highly sought after for the commercial food market, these animals rarely get to a ripe old age. They can live over 25 years and reach 1m (3ft 3in) in length.

5 SPINY LOBSTER
Palinurus elephas
This is a large spiny lobster in shades of orange and red with a sharp spiny carapace and abdomen. Growing over 50cm (1ft 8in) in length, it lives in caverns and rocky crevices. It is more active at night. It guards its lair, standing at the entrance on stout, long, striped legs with its huge, long, sensory antenna protruding into open water. Very timid in character, it is commercially fished by traditional lobster pot. Breeding occurs in September and like all lobsters, the female carries the eggs under her abdomen with specially adapted feet.

CRABS
HERMIT CRABS

6 RED HERMIT CRAB
Dardanus calidus
One of the larger hermit crabs to be found, at over 2.5cm (1in), it is instantly recognized by its bright red coloration, green eyes set out on long stalks and orange antennae. It is often associated with the parasitic anemone *Calliactis parasitica*, which it lugs around on the back of its heavy shell home.

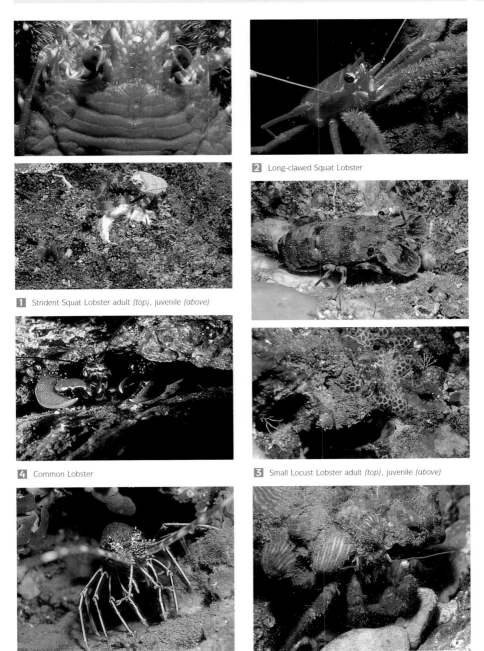

2 Long-clawed Squat Lobster

1 Strident Squat Lobster adult *(top)*, juvenile *(above)*

4 Common Lobster

3 Small Locust Lobster adult *(top)*, juvenile *(above)*

5 Spiny Lobster

6 Red Hermit Crab

1 SEDENTARY HERMIT CRAB
Calcinus tubularis
Curiously, it is only the female of this species that is sedentary in nature, preferring to live in old worm snail holes. The male is much more errant. Slim in body, it is more commonly found inhabiting empty cowrie shells. It grows up to 10mm (½in), has long stalked eyes, is reddish-brown in colour with pale striped legs and has pincer arms with red spots.

2 STRIPED HERMIT CRAB
Pagarus anachoretus
This species is fairly recognizable by its overall brownish coloration and white to bluish stripes and bands over all of its legs and pincer arms. It also has relatively few hairs on its legs, but they are long. Its antenna are also long and banded with white. Its body length is 2.5cm (1in).

3 HAIRY HERMIT CRAB
Pagarus cuanensis
This is quite a small and distinct species, growing to 1.5cm (½in) and is characterized by its extremely hairy lower legs and pincers, which always appear to be clogged up with bits of detritus. Overall brown in colour, it has long, stalked, pale blue eyes and brown-and-white striped antennae.

4 PRIDEAUX'S HERMIT CRAB
Pagarus prideux
This species is mainly associated with the commensal anemone *Adamsia carciniapados*, which completely envelops its carrier shell. The crab is speckled with white and tinged with mauve and is overall a light tan in colour with pinkish striped legs and striped eye stalks. It grows up to 3cm (1¼in) long. The females lay eggs throughout the summer season. They are bright gold and are kept in the shelly home until the larvae are freed by the crab, climbing out of the anemone-covered shell, endangering its softer body parts.

OTHER CRABS

5 MASKED CRAB
Corystes cassivelaunus
This soft sand- and mud-living crab grows to around 7.5cm (3in) in length and has two long antennae, which form a breathing tube when the crab is hidden under the surface. Coloured a uniform light tan or pale cream, the carapace is roughly triangular in shape. The pincer arms or chelipeds are very long in the male and short and stout in the female.

6 SPONGE CRAB
Dromia personata
A muddy brown in colour and covered in fine hairs, the Sponge Crab lives in low light areas generally in caverns or caves, where it sometimes places a sponge on its back for additional camouflage. Growing over 7cm (2¾in), it is quite a stout crab with strong limbs and pincers, which have pinkish tips.

7 ANEMONE SPIDER CRAB
Inachus phalangium
Commonly associated with the Snakelocks Anemone *Anemonia sulcata*, this spider crab enjoys the protection of the anemone, being seemingly immune to its stinging tentacles. It is only the female of the species that lives in the anemone. Brownish in colour, it is often covered in fine hairs and bits of algae and sponge to help in camouflage. It only leaves the anemone at night to feed but stays close by. It grows to 5cm (2in) in length.

8 SPINY SPIDER CRAB
Herbstia condyliata
This small species grows to only 3cm (1¼in) and is widely distributed. An active scavenger, it only comes out at night and prefers underhanging rock faces dotted with small holes. The legs are striped and it is of an overall reddish-brown colour.

1 Sedentary Hermit Crab

2 Striped Hermit Crab *(above)*

4 Prideaux's Hermit Crab *(below)*

3 Hairy Hermit Crab

5 Masked Crab *(above)*

6 Sponge Crab *(right)*

7 Anemone Spider Crab

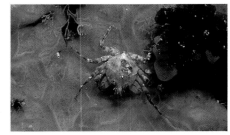

8 Spiny Spider Crab

1 RED SPIDER CRAB
Lissa chiragra
Rarely seen, and then only at night, the Red Spider Crab grows to only 5cm (2in) and is quite happy on rocky substrates or amidst Posidonia. Brilliant red in colour, it is also characterized by the nodular outgrowths on its carapace and at each of the joints on its legs.

2 COMMON SPIDER CRAB
Maja crispata
A master of camouflage, this crab lives in most habitats and fastens bits of algae and sometimes sponge all over its carapace, legs and pincers. Owing to its fairly sedentary nature and not moving when it senses danger, it is very rarely seen as it is often so overgrown that it resembles a lump of seaweed-covered rock. It can grow to over 7cm (2¾in) and is sold commercially for the meat contained within its carapace.

ECHINODERMS
Phylum Echinodermata

This important phylum is entirely marine in origin and has many different family groups. Completely varied in form, they nevertheless all have common characteristics, such as calcareous plates, a water vascular system and tiny tube feet for locomotion and capturing food. Many are armed with some degree of protection. Most obvious of all are the sea urchins, which are surrounded by sharp spines.

BRITTLESTARS

3 BLACK BRITTLESTAR
Ophiocomino nigra
Fairly common in deeper water and not always black in colour as the name would suggest, this brittlestar has five to seven rows of short spines along each arm. Its arms are up to 10cm (4in) long. Feeding on detritus deposits, it is omnivorous and can occur in large numbers.

4 LONG-ARMED BRITTLESTAR
Ophioderma longicauda
This species has a circular disc, which is often patterned and up to 2.5cm (1in) in diameter with arms as long as 15cm (6in). Each arm has small rows of blunt spines. This species prefers low light and is most often found deep inside caves and caverns or in very deep water.

5 FRAGILE BRITTLESTAR
Ophiothrix fragilis
This is a colourful species with the disc and arms coming in almost every colour imaginable and often varied on each individual. Hairy in appearance, the arms, which grow up to 6.3cm (2½in) long, are characterized by having numerous rows of quite long spines. It can occur in extremely dense beds in deep water.

CRINOIDS

6 FEATHER STARFISH
Antedon mediterranea
This characteristically shaped crinoid has a tiny body with the mouth on the upper surface of the cup and surrounded by ten long flexible arms up to 10cm (4in) long, which have slender lateral branches. Under the cup-like body are a number of flexible feet or cirri with which it holds on. Usually reddish-orange in colour and sometimes with banded arms, it is commonly found on wrecks and likes strong current or well-aerated water.

2 Common Spider Crab

1 Red Spider Crab *(above)*

3 Black Brittlestar *(right)*

4 Long-armed Brittlestar *(below)*

5 Fragile Brittlestar *(bottom left)*

6 Feather Starfish *(bottom right)*

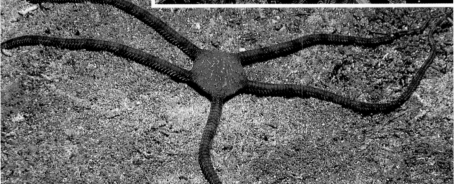

STARFISH

1 BURROWING STARFISH
Astropecten irregularis
This is a fairly large burrowing starfish growing up to 20cm (8in) with five distinct arms. It is a pale cream in colour and is a uniform texture with the upper surface covered in paxillae. It has well-defined marginal plates bearing short, erect spines. It is found on fine sand and is usually partially or wholly buried. It feeds on small bivalves, worms and crustaceans.

2 IRREGULAR STARFISH
Coscinasterias tenuispina
This species can have 6–12 arms, often of different lengths, probably owing to damage inflicted whilst the starfish is young and its ability to regenerate limbs. It is usually light cream in colour, but mottled with brown, red and even bluish or purple blotches. Growing to around 20cm (8in) in diameter, it is found in most habitats and feeds on the rich algae found in shallow water.

3 RED STAR
Echinaster sepositus
This is a very common, rough-skinned, red starfish with five, pointed, circular-sectioned arms up to 18cm (7in) long. The rough skin is actually papulae or gill structures and it has a slimy feel. Found in most depths, it feeds on various algae.

4 SPINY STARFISH
Marthasterias glacialis
One of the largest of the starfish found in these waters, it has five, very long, subcylindrical arms that are roughly tapering and covered in longitudinal rows of thick, sharp spines. Each spine is surrounded by a raised group of pedicellariae. This species prefers a rocky substrate and is mottled greenish-brown in colour. It grows to over 70cm (2ft 4in) in diameter.

5 LONG-LIMB STARFISH
Ophidiaster ophidianus
Probably the most brilliantly coloured of the large starfish found, this species has long, cylindrical, blunt-tipped arms, which vary from red in colour to even more brilliant red, violet or orange. It can grow to over 50cm (1ft 8in) in diameter and is quite rough in texture with a slightly fuzzy appearance.

SEA URCHINS

6 BLACK SEA URCHIN
Arbacia lixula
Once thought to be the male version of the Rock Sea Urchin (*see* p.82), the Black Sea Urchin enjoys a well-lit, soft rock habitat where it burrows into the rock whilst eating the algae, which grow into the recess. It grows to around 8cm (3¼in) in diameter and has a black shell with black spines.

7 SEA POTATO
Echinocardium cordatum
The common name refers to the brittle empty test or shell, which is sometimes seen on the sandy seabed or shore. The animal when alive is covered in a mat of fine, cream spines almost like hairs. Slightly heart-shaped, fairly round and up to 7.5cm (3in) across, it burrows in the fine sand and is a deposit feeder.

8 PURPLE HEART URCHIN
Spatangus purpureus
Also heart-shaped, it can grow as large as 12cm (4¾in) and is coloured a brilliant purple with light, fine spines. It only burrows shallowly and prefers coarse sand and shell gravel.

1 Burrowing Starfish

2 Irregular Starfish

3 Red Star

4 Spiny Starfish

5 Long-limb Starfish

6 Black Sea Urchin

7 Sea Potato

8 Purple Heart Urchin

1 LONG-SPINED URCHIN
Centrostephanus longispinus
This species is relatively rare in the Mediterranean, having been almost wiped out a few years ago by a virulent disease. Unmistakably recognizable by its long dark spines up to 13cm (5in) long, which are sometimes banded, this sea urchin prefers low light conditions and is usually seen in deep water.

2 ROCK SEA URCHIN
Paracentrotus lividus
One of the most common sea urchins in the western and central Mediterranean, it occurs in a variety of colour forms and has a rather flattened round test or shell. Growing to around 7cm (2¾in) in diameter, it burrows into soft limestone, leaving cavities in the rock wall, which it enlarges as it grows. It is a herbivore, feeding on algae around its hole or over rocky surfaces.

3 VIOLET SEA URCHIN
Sphaerechinus granularis
This is a large globular sea urchin growing to around 13cm (5¼in) in diameter and coloured a vivid purple. Usually with white-tipped spines, it is often all the one colour. It likes open, well-lit ground where it browses on algae and has the habit of attaching small pieces of detritus, shell fragments or algae to its spines for camouflage.

SEA CUCUMBERS

4 COTTON SPINNER
Holothuria forskåli
The most common of the cucumbers, this species comes in two colours, either jet black or varied tan and brown with brown spots on a cream base. Its name comes from its defence mechanism when it ejects sticky, white thread when threatened. It can reach over 20cm (8in) in length and has a dense, tubercle-covered body and numerous tube feet. Feeding on sand and mud particles, which it ingests and passes through its body cavity, the excreta is usually recognized easily as it resembles an egg-like necklace chain made of fine sand particles.

5 WHITE SPOT CUCUMBER
Holothuria polii
Also distinctively coloured, this species is black or dark brown in colour and is covered in tiny, white, spot-like spines. It grows to around 20cm (8in) and is an active detritus browser.

6 TUBULAR CUCUMBER
Holothuria tubulosa
The longest of the sea cucumbers found commonly, the Tubular Cucumber can grow over 30cm (12in) long and is varicoloured with dark brown on the top and light brown to peach shades on its flanks. It has conspicuous, pointed tubercles all over its body and prefers to live at the base of cliffs and amongst seagrass beds.

ASCIDIANS

Ascidians, also referred to as tunicates or sea squirts, give the appearance of being very simple animals. Yet they are very closely related to vertebrates as they do possess a gut and intestine and a rod-like structure similar to the vertebrate backbone. They are either solitary or occur in large communal groups. Some even form large colonial formations.

7 CONICAL TUNICATE
Aplidium conicum
This ball-shaped structure grows to around 20cm (8in) across and has numerous small apertures all over the body. Coloured almost translucent white to cream, it has less the characteristic of an ascidian and more resembles a sponge.

1   Long-spined urchin

2   Rock Sea Urchin

3   Violet Sea Urchin

4   Cotton Spinner

5   White Spot Cucumber

6   Tubular Cucumber

7   Conical Tunicate

1 CIONA
Ciona intestinalis
Usually found on its own, this sea squirt grows to approximately 15cm (6in). It has a white or translucent body with lobed ends to its siphons. These lobes may also be tinged with bright yellow. The inhalant opening is on the top and the exhalant is about a third of the way down on the side. In colder waters, this large species is often associated with *Ascidiella aspersa*, another similarly sized tunicate. Their range covers the whole of the north Atlantic, but they are found especially in the Scottish sea lochs and southern Norway. Ciona is found from the lower shore, down to 500m (1,650 ft) and grows on rocks, boulder cliffs and algae. It is particularly fond of man-made structures, such as piers, shipwrecks and buoys, and it is thought that its very widespread distribution is due to its propensity to attach itself to ships' hulls. It reproduces throughout the year once it reaches over 2cm (¾in) in height.

2 BLUESTRIPED LIGHT BULB TUNICATE
Clavelina dellavallei
This is the largest of a distinctive small group of sea squirts. Growing singularly, but in association with other individuals, it grows to around 2.5cm (1in) high. Tinged with blue lines and a yellow internal ribbing, it is unmistakable.

3 LIGHT BULB TUNICATE
Clavelina lepadiformis
A very similar species to the Bluestriped, this sea squirt grows in small attached colonies and is around 1.5cm (½in) tall with distinctive, white, light bulb filament markings within the transparent body cavity. It should not be confused with the Ball Tunicate, where the individuals are tightly packed together to form a ball shape; Light Bulb Tunicate colonies are much more loose, almost to the point of having individual zooids. These zooids are cylindrical and smooth, and you may be able to spot either amber- or red-coloured eggs or tadpole-shaped larvae within the body cavity. This species is occasionally found in deeper rock pools, but it is generally more associated with harbour walls, vertical cliffs and ledges.

4 GLASS BELL TUNICATE
Clavelina nana
The smallest of the bell tunicates at only 7mm (¼in) high, it grows in loose aggregations on algae fronds and around the base of sea fans. Stalked and creamy white in colour, its body has horizontal lines patterned throughout.

5 DENDRODOA
Dendrodoa spp.
This small orange or red sea squirt, only 8mm (¼in) in size, prefers low light but well-aerated conditions and can form quite large colonial patches. Slightly fuzzy in appearance, both siphons are next to each other. It is commonly associated with various hydroids, which grow amidst the colony. *Dendrodoa* species are also the tunicates most commonly associated with the sponge *Clathrina*, where the lacy network formations tend to weave their way amongst the small bells of the tunicate.

6 BALL TUNICATE
Diozone violacea
This is a tightly packed group of individuals, which resemble *Clavelina lepadiformis* in structure, but here they are grouped together to form a ball reaching 20cm (8in) in height and over 40cm (1ft 4in) in diameter.

7 SEA POTATO
Halocinthya papillosa
This is the most distinctive of the ascidians and individuals are usually a deep red colour. Some individuals may be a pale pink in deeper caves, but the siphons are still tinged dark red. It prefers a solitary existence and grows to around 12cm (4¾in).

1 Ciona

2 Bluestriped Light Bulb Tunicate

3 Light Bulb Tunicate

4 Glass Bell Tunicate

5 Dendrodoa *(left)*

6 Ball Tunicate *(below)*

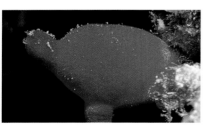

7 Sea Potato

SHARKS

There are two family groups of fish, the elasmobranchs, which are cartilaginous and include all the sharks and rays and the teleosts, which are all other bony fishes.

Sharks are a highly specialized and ancient family present in the Mediterranean and although the species are principally represented by the cat sharks, which are not harmful to man, there are great white sharks to be found. All sharks eat living animals, but many also eat decaying matter. Most are active hunters at night and all are shy. They are able to detect low-level electrical currents and can find sleeping fish at night. With highly developed sensory ampullae, they are able to detect low-frequency vibrations from great distances as well as scent from injured or dying animals.

1 SAND TIGER SHARK
Carcharias taurus

The Sand Tiger Shark or Ragged-tooth Shark, up to 3.30m (11ft) long, prefers deeper water where it feeds on a variety of bony fish and crustaceans. Although very fearsome looking, it is not known to attack man. The species is now collected commercially for the aquarium trade as it has been found to be particularly suitable for large enclosed environments, such as sealife centres or public aquariums. There are problems associated with the transport and health of these sharks and a number of aquariums have reported fatalities. Conservation bodies are against this trade in sharks. *Ecology:* Regularly seen in the eastern Mediterranean during late summer, particularly off the coast of Lebanon, Syria and southern Turkey where it can occur quite close inshore near vertical cliffs and deep reefs. Denser than water, it is known to swallow air at the surface to help its buoyancy.

2 SMOOTH HOUND
Mustelus mustelus

Growing to around 1.60m (5ft 4in), this small, smooth-skinned shark has large eyes and a long and slender body with a sharply pointed snout and five gills. The species has two large, almost equal-sized, dorsal fins and unlike the Spurdog, has an anal fin. Its main prey species are bony fish, squid and octopus, and small crustaceans. *Ecology:* The species likes bottom-living and tends to stay in deep water during the day and rises into shallow waters around the coastline at night to feed.

3 BLUE SHARK
Prionace glauca

This shark grows to 3m (10ft), has a slender body, wing-like pectoral fins, long snout and large eyes, and is blue in colour. At night the colour changes slightly to a greenish shade. It feeds on small fish and squid rounding up the schools and attacking fiercely. Largely under threat by man, it is caught by drift net and 'sport' anglers. *Ecology:* This is a pelagic shark, often working in small groups as it hunts around inshore shoals of fish. Blue Sharks are the widest ranging of all cartilaginous fish, being found in all tropical and temperate waters. Tagged individuals from the Canary Islands have been found in Cuba and individuals from the USA have been captured in Gibraltar, indicating that they use the equatorial currents in their migration patterns.

4 LESSER-SPOTTED DOGFISH
Scyliorhinus canicula

Although this is referred to as a 'dogfish' it is actually in the cat shark family and is perhaps the most common of all the species encountered in the region. Rarely over 1m (3ft 3in) in length, its body is rough to the touch and is covered in dark spots and blotches. *Ecology:* It is common in shallow waters and lays its eggs from May right through to September when it attaches its 'mermaid's purse' egg case by four long flexible tendrils to various sea fans. Depending on the location and amount of plankton in the water, these egg cases gradually become covered in marine life, further protecting the delicate embryo inside.

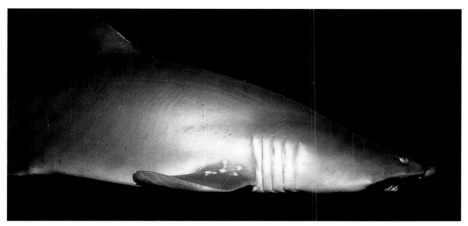

1 Sand Tiger Shark

2 Smooth Hound

3 Blue Shark

4 Lesser-spotted Dogfish

1 NURSE HOUND
Scyliorhinus stellaris

Very similar to the Lesser-spotted Dogfish, this is a much larger species, growing to almost 2m (6ft 6in). A purely nocturnal feeder, it preys on octopus, molluscs, crustaceans and demersal fish. *Ecology*: This species is hunted for use in aquariums as it is sedentary of nature and requires little work to keep it happy!

2 ANGEL SHARK
Squatina squatina

Growing to around 1.80m (6ft), this is a nocturnal bottom-dweller, more like a large ray than a shark. Roughly diamond-shaped, it has large, fleshy pectoral fins and a rounded snout with a speckled body. *Ecology*: It is generally buried in sand and stalks fish in this way, lying in wait until fish pass close to the large mouth. It opens its mouth wide, whilst lunging upwards, drawing the hapless prey into its mouth. It is quite harmless to humans and generally fearless of divers.

3 SPURDOG
Squalus acanthias

Very similar in shape and appearance to the Smooth Hound, this small shark is distinguished by an obvious spur or spike directly attached and in front of the dorsal fin. The males reach over 1m (3ft 3in) in length, whilst the females are much smaller at 75cm (2ft 6in). *Ecology*: Fairly slow moving, it migrates from deeper waters into shallow estuaries during the summer months to have its young.

RAYS

Rays are instantly distinguishable as their pectoral fins are joined onto the head and form a broad skirt around the body. They have a cartilaginous skeleton like the sharks, but have no dorsal fins and their mouth parts are on the underside.

4 COMMON STINGRAY
Dasyatis pastinaca

Widely distributed but quite rare, the Common Stingray, growing to 60cm (2ft), is found locally in most areas of the region. It prefers a sandy bottom and quite often lives near the base of cliffs. *Ecology*: Described from Ancient Greek times, it has one or more barbed spines at the base of its tail, which can be whipped forward and plunged into a predator in a purely defensive posture.

5 HONEYCOMB WHIPRAY
Himantura uarnak

A Lessepsian migrant through the Red Sea, this large ray is steadily spreading through the Mediterranean. *Ecology:* This species can grow to 1.50m (5ft) in diameter. The distinctive blending of the spots over its back into a honeycomb pattern is easily recognized. It has an extremely long tail, up to twice the body length. The body pattern gradually fades as the animal matures.

6 THORNBACK RAY
Raja clavata

The species grows up to 90cm (3ft) and has a roughly diamond shape with a pattern of light spots over a uniform olive-green to light-brown body colour. It is characterized by having a series of short spines down its back and along its tail. *Ecology*: This is quite a common ray. It prefers deeper water where it lives on a fine sand and gravel seabed. It hunts for small demersal fish, molluscs and crustaceans and is usually caught in trawl nets as a by-catch.

1 Nurse Hound

2 Angel Shark

3 Spurdog *(above)*; egg case *(below left)*

4 Common Stingray *(right)*

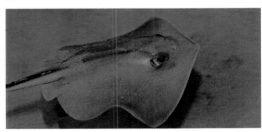

5 Honeycomb Whipray

6 Thornback ray

1 FOUR-EYED RAY
Raja miraletus

Another migrant from the Atlantic, this easily recognized ray grows to 60cm (2ft) and has two or four distinctive dark spots on its back. Fairly common in all sandy areas, it is commercially caught and is commonly seen in fish markets. *Ecology*: Often seen on early evening and night dives, when it is an active predator feeding in pairs.

2 ELECTRIC RAY
Torpedo marmorata

These fish are easily recognized by their round-shaped body and thick fleshy tail. It is important to recognize the species, as a shock from the fish can stun a man. Light brown with a mottled or marbled appearance, the eyes are set far forward on the head with a pair of lobed spiracles directly behind the eyes. It grows to 60cm (2ft) long. *Ecology:* Prey are stunned when the ray folds its wings around the subject and stuns it with an electric shock, recorded at 220 volts at 8 amps. This species is solitary and nocturnal, tending to hide under the sand during the day.

EELS

3 CONGER EEL
Conger conger

The Conger Eel is greyish-blue in colour, cylindrical and can grow over 2m (6ft 8in) in length. It has a scaleless, snake-like body with a single long dorsal fin, which merges into the tail and anal fins. It has large strong jaws and enjoys a diet of crustaceans and small fish. *Ecology:* The Conger Eel is common throughout the entire region and is an inquisitive fish, tending to live in caverns or rocky crevices. It is also found regularly on shipwrecks where there is always an abundance of long, fish-shaped pipes to hide in. Little is known of its breeding habits, but it is known to migrate into deep-water spawning grounds where several thousand eggs are laid by each fish. Similar in ecology to the Common Eel *Anguilla anguilla*, the young take two to three years to return to the inshore habitat.

4 SERPENT EEL
Ophisunus serpens

Ovoid in shape, the species grows to around 45cm (1ft 6in) long and has a light tan body with numerous brown spots at the front of the head. The eyes are close together at the front of the snout, which is quite long with a sharp teeth-filled jaw. *Ecology:* This quite rare fish hides under the sand during day and pokes its head out at night time, when it lies in wait for passing food species, such as small shrimps and fish.

5 MORAY EEL
Muraena helena

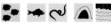

The Mediterranean Moray Eel can grow over 1.50m (5ft) and is one of the favourite fish for divers to find. The species is characterized by having quite a small head, brown in colour, and tan spots, which develop into broader golden markings on the flanks of the body. It has a long dorsal and anal fin, which merge into the rounded tail with no pectoral fins. The outer edge of the fin is spotted with either white or gold colours. *Ecology:* Occurring on shallow reefs and wrecks all round the coast, this species tends to come out at night to feed and will hide in a protective hole during the day. It usually has a few symbiotic shrimps also living in the same hole, which keep the fish clean of parasites.

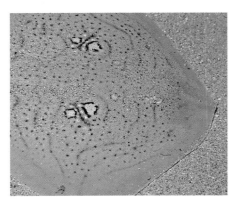

1 Four-eyed Ray

2 Electric Ray

3 Conger Eel

4 Serpent Eel

5 Moray Eel

PIPEFISH
Family Sygnathidae

1 LONG-SNOUT SEA HORSE
Hippocampus ramulosus

In Roman mythology, Neptune's chariot was drawn by beautiful white sea horses and their name is from the Greek *hippos* meaning 'horse' and *kampe* meaning 'worm' or 'caterpillar'. This curious fish has a horse-shaped head set at an angle to the body, the trunk of which is generally short and fat tapering to a long prehensile tail. It grows to a maximum of 15cm (6in) and is usually found in its life-long mating pairs. Sea horses feed on small shrimp and other tiny planktonic crustacea, picking at them with their long snouts 'hoovering' them into their mouths. *Ecology:* Sea horses enjoy algae-covered rocks and seagrass meadows in well-illuminated and aerated water. They move infrequently making them difficult to spot and owing to their nature of having bits of algae on their long fringed 'mane', this only enhances their already excellent camouflage.

2 PIPEFISH
Sygnathus acus

Pipefish are a closely related species to sea horses and, as the name implies, grow long and thin with tube-like bodies over 45cm (1ft 6in) long. The snout is more than half of the head length and there is a distinct lump on the head behind the eyes. The body is ridged with obvious scaly plates. The dorsal fin is set near the rear of the body and has no anal or pelvic fins. *Ecology:* Seen fairly regularly throughout the region, they are however difficult to spot as they lie along algae fronds, rendering them almost invisible.

SNIPEFISH
Family Macrohamphodidae

3 SNIPEFISH
Macrohamphosus scolopax

This is a curiously shaped fish, unmistakable with its compressed body and elongated snout. Swimming in small groups, snout downwards, it hunts for small crustaceans, worms and fish fry around the deeper coral reefs. Generally inhabiting muddy or soft sandy areas, it is often associated with sea pens. *Ecology:* The Snipefish has a tiny mouth at the end of a long snout in front of large conspicuous eyes and is usually only found in depths greater than about 25m (80ft).

LIZARDFISH
Family Synodontidae

4 LIZARDFISH
Synodus saurus

The Lizardfish has a cylindrical body with a wide, slightly upturned head and a wide mouth absolutely jammed full of teeth. It has two dorsal fins, one very large, which it folds back against the body, the other tiny, and it grows to 40cm (1ft 4in) in length. It has a light tan and mottled brown appearance which helps its camouflage when it dives for cover into the sand. *Ecology:* It is common in shallow sandy areas where it hides under the sand. Quite often, all that is seen are the two eyes and the upturned mouth.

2 Pipefish *(above)*

1 Long-snout Sea Horse *(left)*

3 Snipefish

4 Lizardfish

ANGLERFISH
Family Lophidae

1 ANGLERFISH
Lophius piscatorius

The Anglerfish or monkfish is unmistakable by its large flattened body and incredibly ugly visage (unless you are another anglerfish!). Growing to over 2m (6ft 6in), it has a huge head surrounded by a frill of fleshy appendages around the lower jaw. The mouth is filled with sharp inward-pointing teeth and when fully extended, the mouth is virtually circular. Behind the head are a row of adapted dorsal fin rays, which it uses to dangle in front of its mouth to 'angle' for its dinner. *Ecology:* Sedentary by nature, the Anglerfish has two very strong ventral fins, which have been adapted into feet, which can thrust the fish rapidly off the seabed in either fight, flight or catching food. When lying in wait, the fish lures other prey species into its catchment area, then with a combination of thrust and opening its mouth wide, sea water is sucked into the cavity along with the poor dinner!

SCORPIONFISH
Family Scorpaenidae

Scorpionfish are rather stout fish, bottom dwelling with no swimbladders for flotation. All are armed with venomous dorsal fins and have sharp spikes to their gill covers. They usually have warty protuberances to help in their camouflage and are opportunistic predators. They sit still near aggregations of small fish, lying in wait for the food to swim close enough to catch.

2 SMALL ROCKFISH
Scorpaena notata

This small species only grows to 20cm (8in) and is fairly free of any facial cutaneous protrusions. It is variable bright red and orange with yellowish and brown blotches and shows a black mark on the dorsal fin when it displays. *Ecology:* This species prefers low light conditions and can be more often seen at night when the diver's torch light can pick out the brilliant colours against the rocky or algae-covered background. It likes the entrances to caverns where it can be seen upside down or high up on the cliff wall.

3 BROWN SCORPIONFISH
Scorpaena porcus

This stout species is slightly larger than the Small Rockfish at 30cm (1ft) and has a much more universal colouring of dark brown, often speckled with cream or light brownish blotches. It has several large, backward-facing spines around the gill covers and there are two large, fleshy protuberances above the eyes. *Ecology:* This species prefers more open water in well-illuminated areas such as seagrass meadows where it lies in wait for its prey to swim by close to its mouth. Their spiny coverings are purely defensive and I have witnessed an Anglerfish spitting this fish out when it tried to eat it.

4 GREAT ROCKFISH
Scorpaena scrofa

This is the largest of the Mediterranean scorpionfish and can grow over 50cm (1ft 8in). More tan and light brown in colour, it has many fleshy appendices underneath the jaw and around the head, helping it to blend into the background for additional camouflage. *Ecology:* It is found in most habitats, but prefers well-lit areas around seagrass meadows and amidst a jumble of algae-covered boulders.

1 Anglerfish *(above)*   2 Small Rockfish *(below)*

3 Brown Scorpionfish

4 Great Rockfish

GROUPERS
Family Serranidae

The grouper family has few representatives in the region and has been hunted mercilessly for many years by fishermen. The flesh is highly prized and when you consider that some larger specimens can weigh several hundred kilos, you can understand the greed that is attached to the catch. Thankfully there are many established marine parks where the largest of the grouper are still abundant. They hunt by rushing at their victims with their mouths open, sucking in the prey. All fish start as females and change into males as they get older. This could upset the development of the species if the larger fish get caught.

1 SWALLOWTAIL SEAPERCH
Anthias anthias

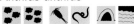

This is a wonderfully coloured anthias from which all the other species descriptions are derived. It grows to around 10cm (4in) and is pink to red in colour with long pelvic fins, which are rounded and tinged with yellow. The tail is long and tapering and the adult male has an extended dorsal spine, which is bright yellow. It also has variable markings around the eyes and snout. *Ecology:* All fish in the small schools are females except for the largest one which is the male. Like many other species of fish, when the male dies, the predominant female changes sex and changes into a male. It inhabits deeper caves and caverns and prefers low light. Large numbers of them can also be found on deeper shipwrecks.

2 SEA BASS
Dicentrarchus labrax

Extremely popular for the commercial market, this silvery grey fish is common in coastal waters and grows to around 1m (3ft 3in). It is also farmed for the export market and likes sandy, muddy or rocky coasts. *Ecology:* Sea Bass live in small groups and whilst the young feed on most types of sea creatures, the adults hunt exclusively for fish. They like offshore islands and are to be observed fairly close to the surface.

3 DUSKY GROUPER
Epinephelus marginatus

Although this grouper grows to a similar adult size of 1.50m (5ft), it is the Dusky Grouper which is so representative of the best of what the Mediterranean has to offer. Very popular with divers, it can be quite territorial, yet also tolerates large numbers whenever there is food available, such as feeding time in some marine parks. The Dusky Grouper is rich brown in colour and mottled with pale cream spots and blotches. *Ecology:* Friendly and inquisitive, the larger males will approach divers out of curiosity and can live for up to 50 years.

4 STRIPED GROUPER
Epinephelus costae

A smaller species, growing to around 1m (3ft 3in) and rarely over this, the Striped Grouper is also referred to as the 'Goldblotch Grouper'. It has distinctive brown or golden horizontal stripes over a rather dull body colour. *Ecology:* This fish enjoys shipwrecks and deeper water and becomes a fully mature female at 40cm (1ft 4in) long. It also changes into a male at 60cm (2ft), making it vulnerable to spear fishermen.

5 CANINE GROUPER
Epinephelus caninus

This species can grow to 1.50m (5ft), but in general only smaller ones are seen, around 50–75cm (1ft 8in–2ft 6in). Pale grey to tan in colour with a few blotched markings, it is quite timid and prefers deeper water and rocky reefs. *Ecology:* The Canine Grouper is so named because of its strongly developed teeth, which it uses to catch and crush crustaceans. It is usually seen on its own and has a large territory, chasing others of the same species away aggressively.

1 Swallowtail Seaperch

2 Sea Bass

3 Dusky Grouper

4 Striped Grouper

5 Canine Grouper

1 BLACK TAIL COMBER
Serranus atricauda

A smaller member of the family and an inter-loper from the Atlantic, the Black Tail Comber is more readily seen in the western Mediter-ranean. It grows to 35cm (1ft 2in) in length and is varied in colour, often with dark squarish patches and a broad horizontal line along its flanks. *Ecology:* This is a territorial fish, vicious-ly defending its territory, and can be found in fairly shallow waters of less than 25m (80ft) around seagrass meadows and rocky reefs.

2 COMBER
Serranus cabrilla

The Comber grows to around 30cm (1ft) and is pale in colour with reddish-brown vertical bands and stripes. It has a well-defined jaw and is char-acterized by a sawed edge of its anterior gill cov-ers. *Ecology:* This friendly species can be found in very shallow water, particularly around small rocky reefs at the shoreline. It enjoys Posidonia seagrass meadows as well as small rocky walls, where it darts for cover when it realizes just how large divers are!

3 PAINTED COMBER
Serranus scriba

Many divers instantly recognize this fish due to its very inquisitive nature and fairly gaudy col-oration, which make it the most obvious of the *Serranus* species. It can grow to around 35cm (1ft 2in) and has distinctive markings around the face, with a broad dark stripe, which runs from the snout through the eye. The body has vertical, dark stripes of variable length and has a pro-nounced blue spot to its belly. *Ecology:* Found in water, as shallow as 1m (3ft 3in), this fish prefers a rocky reef filled with small holes where it cannot only hide, but can also feed on the other inhabi-tants of these holes. This small member of the grouper family is also synonymous with Posidonia seagrass beds, where it patrols the periphery in search of small crustaceans and fish fry.

CARDINALFISH
Family Apogonidae

4 CARDINALFISH
Apogon imberbis

Well known to all divers who visit the Mediter-ranean, the Cardinalfish is very common on all reefs and is instantly recognizable. It is oval in shape, grows to around 10cm (4in), and is a uni-form reddish-orange colour with a vertical, dark line, which extends from the snout to the gill cov-ers; the eyes have two horizontal stripes to deline-ate the stripe. *Ecology:* Cardinalfish are always seen in large groups at the entrances to caves or large holes in the cliff face where they shelter during daylight hours. At night, they disperse into open water to feed on rising plankton. After spawning, the male takes the egg mass of about 20,000 eggs into its mouth for protection. To provide ventilation, it chews the eggs carefully in its huge distended jaws. Whilst in this brooding phase, the males are unable to take any nour-ishment until after the eggs hatch and are released into the wild. Although highly advanta-geous in the protection of the young against any predators, it is particularly stressful on the fish. This small fish is very wide ranging and is found from the shores of the Lebanon to Portugal, the Azores and Cape Verde Islands.

1 Black Tail Comber; adult *(above)*, juvenile *(above right)*

2 Comber

3 Painted Comber

4 Cardinalfish

JACKS
Family Carrangidae

Jacks are a highly specialized, powerful swimming fish, more at home in the open ocean than near the shore. All have very streamlined bodies with a narrow tail base and forked tail. The pectoral fins are scythe shaped and most species look like the tuna family, although much slimmer. Most of the species are fish hunters and are themselves an important source of food for human consumption.

1 BLUE RUNNER
Caranx crysos

This species of jack generally grows to around 35cm (1ft 2in) and has a distinctive arched lateral line. Silvery reflective, it gives a blue appearance and is a creature of the open ocean. *Ecology:* It is rarely seen close to shore but will frequent offshore reefs which have vertical walls. It hunts along the walls in small packs, rounding up smaller shoals of sardines and the like, before attacking them in an organized frenzy.

2 CREVALLE JACK
Caranx hippos

Growing to around 60cm (2ft), it is very rare that this fish attains a larger size owing to overfishing. It is a highly prized species. All members of the species share a common shape. *Ecology:* Crevalle Jacks only form groups when they are young and rarely venture inshore. Adults are solitary and wide ranging throughout the region.

3 MEDITERRANEAN AMBERJACK
Seriola carpenteri

These amberjacks grow to around 45cm (1ft 6in) and, although very similar to the Great Amberjack, this species is distinguished by the much lighter yellowish markings on the head and along the flanks. The pectoral and anal fins are also tinged yellow. *Ecology:* Little is known of its distribution, but it feeds on squid and small fish which are hunted in small packs.

4 GREAT AMBERJACK
Seriola dumerili

Growing to over 1.50m (5ft), the Great Amberjack has a distinctive dark flash of yellow or tan, which traverses the eye and spreads along the top of the body. It hunts in small packs and is hunted by other jacks and even Barracuda. *Ecology:* The hunting packs work quite close to the edge of the reef and around shipwrecks, rounding up schools of smelt and bogue before attacking with lightning speed.

BARRACUDA
Family Sphyraenidae

5 BARRACUDA
Sphyraena sphyraena

Growing over 1.60m (5ft 4in), Barracuda are regarded as one of the more successful predators in our oceans and are frequently seen in large groups near offshore reefs and rocky cliffs. They like areas of strong moving current, particularly where diverging currents meet, carrying food species their way. They only go solo when reaching maturity and it is said that these mature fish are much more dangerous. *Ecology:* When they rest in diverging currents, barracuda often start to circle each other creating a great moving vortex of fish. The distribution of the species is unclear, as a smaller cousin *Sphyraena viridensis* is very similar to young *Sphyraena sphyraena*.

1 Blue Runner

2 Crevalle Jack

3 Mediterranean Amberjack

4 Great Amberjack with attack wound

5 Barracuda

GREY MULLET
Family Muglidae

1 BOXLIP MULLET
Oedalechilus labeo

Boxlip Mullet are a uniform silvery grey in colour with thin, brownish lines along the flanks and grow to around 25cm (10in). A schooling species, they are seen in most habitats. *Ecology:* They have large, fleshy lips with which they 'hoover' the fine silt layers from rock surface and algae, but more commonly they are seen feeding at the surface on plankton debris and algae scum.

DRUM
Family Sciaenidea

2 BROWN MEAGRE
Sciaena umbra

This fish grows to around 35cm (1ft 2in) and has a robust silvery body. The head is darker in colour and both the pelvis and anal fins have a strong, white front margin against black, making the rest of the fin look almost invisible. *Ecology*: They usually live in pairs. During the mating season from March to August, the male produces a drumming or croaking noise, produced by its swimbladder.

DAMSELFISH
Family Pomacentridae

3 CHROMIS or DAMSELFISH
Chromis chromis

This is the fish that is most encountered by divers in these waters. It ranges throughout the area and prefers a rocky reef close to shore in well-lit, aerated water. It can grow to 15cm (6in) long. Adults are a dull olive-green or grey in colour with obvious scale markings. *Ecology*: The juveniles have fluorescent blue markings on the body and prefer to hide in crevices.

GOATFISH OR MULLET
Family Mullidae

4 STRIPED MULLET
Mullus surmuletus

This is the most commonly seen and recognized of the mullet. Sometimes referred to as Goatfish, the species is variable in colour and ranges from gold or orange with red blotches to pale cream and browns. It is also recognized by its striped dorsal fin and long, sloping head and fleshy lips. It grows to 40cm (1ft 4in). *Ecology*: It has twin fleshy barbels, which it uses in a sweeping motion to excavate in soft sand or mud in search of small worms and molluscs. Usually working in pairs or small groups, it is quite approachable and is highly prized as a food species.

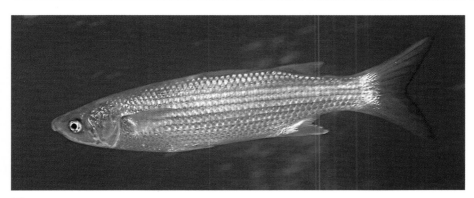

1 Boxlip Mullet

2 Brown Meagre

3 Chromis

4 Striped Mullet

PICAREL
Family Centracanthidae

PICAREL
Spicara maena

A distinctive small fish growing to 25cm (10in). It has quite a high body and is coloured silver with a turquoise top to the flanks and has a distinctive dark blotch midway down its lateral line. *Ecology*: It can occur in large schools around coastal rocky habitats, but at night it rests on the seabed where it makes an easy subject for photography.

SMELT
Family Atherinidae

 SAND SMELT
Atherina hepsetus

Sand Smelt grow to 10cm (4in) and occur in huge coastal schools which they share with Chromis and Bogue. A silvery colour with a bluish hue to the top of the body and a cream midriff, they have a single lateral line down the centre of the narrow tapered body and two short dorsal fins. *Ecology*: They are caught collectively by fishermen lowering large basket nets into the water from the shore.

BREAM
Family Sparidae

The bream are probably the most distinctive of the large families of fish encountered by divers and snorkellers in the Mediterranean. There are at least twenty species to be found. The eleven most common are listed here as they are the species encountered around the coastline and islands. Most are deep-bodied fish and are strong swimmers, always active and covered in fairly visible scales. The colouring is virtually always metallic and the various species are recognized by the combination of blotches, stripes, bands or the lack of those attributes. Most are found in small shoals in mid water or nearby reefs and only the older specimens are encountered singly.

BOGUE
Boops boops

This is a long, silvery fish with a metallic blue upper body and obvious lateral line. Cylindrical in shape, it can grow to 35cm (1ft 2in). It has a fine tapering tail with yellowish, longitudinal lines on the flanks which are not always obvious. *Ecology*: Bogue occur in large feeding schools on shallow reefs and near the surface and are usually mixed in with Sand Smelt and Chromis as they all have a similar diet.

COMMON DENTEX
Dentex dentex

This is a large fish growing to around 1m (3ft 3in) and has a muscular body, compressed laterally. It has a large head and steep forehead, which is slightly darker than the rest of the metallic silvery-grey body. It has obvious silvery lateral lines to the body and a long dorsal fin. *Ecology*: Dentex are usually solitary and are voracious hunters of small fish around shallow reefs, rocky walls and wrecks.

1 Picarel

2 Sand Smelt

3 Bogue

4 Common Dentex

1 BUMP HEAD BREAM
Dentex gibbosus

Also growing to around 1m (3ft 3in) in length, specimens are normally seen at less than half that size around coastal waters owing to over-fishing. Slightly longer than Common Dentex and with a more tapered body, the fish is characterized by a few pale, dotted yellow to golden lines, which run horizontally along its midriff. *Ecology*: It inhabits coastal reefs and hunts near seagrass meadows and is usually seen on its own. Unusually, the young of the species are always male and adult females develop the hump on the front of the head.

2 ANNULAR SEA BREAM
Diplodus annularis

Growing to 24cm (10in), this silvery species is more circular in shape with a dark band around the tale and wide vertical, dull shading just behind the eye from the top of the head to the gill covers. *Ecology*: This fish enjoys coastal reefs and can be found in small groups near sandy bottoms or rocky reefs. The young inhabit brackish waters. Often mistaken for White Bream.

3 ZEBRA BREAM
Diplodus cervinus

A large bream, up to 70cm (2ft) with four or five distinctive olive-green, vertical bands down the plump body. It has a high arched back and steep forehead with a narrow joint at the tail. *Ecology*: Usually seen on its own around rocky reefs and near seagrass meadows.

4 WHITE BREAM
Diplodus sargus sargus

This species is very similar to the Annular Sea Bream for which it is often mistaken. In this fish, there is a black spot at the body side of the tail joint and there are about seven faint, dark, vertical stripes down the body. It grows to 40cm (1ft 4in) and has a high convex forehead with a thick-lipped mouth. *Ecology*: It occurs in large shoals and is territorial on rocky bottoms or near deep crevices at the seabed. It is able to feed on molluscs, crustaceans and sea urchins with its strong jaws and heavy incisors and large crushing molars.

5 TWO-BANDED BREAM
Diplodus vulgaris

The most commonly recognized of the bream, this fish grows to 45cm (1ft 6in). It has two distinctive, vertical, black bands, one behind the eyes, the other before the tail. It has a large head and prominent eyes and the mid-section of the broad flanks has golden yellow lines. *Ecology*: This fish loves seagrass meadows and algae-covered rocks and always occurs in large feeding shoals. It is often associated with other species of wrasse and are unafraid of divers.

6 STRIPED BREAM
Lithognathus mormyrus

The Striped Bream grows to around 55cm (1ft 10in) and is widely distributed throughout all regions. Silver in colour, it has 13–15 distinct, vertical, light gold lines and an obvious high arched lateral line. *Ecology*: This bottom-feeder digs into soft sand looking for worms and small invertebrates and is as at home in brackish water as it is in the sea. All the fish are male at first and then change to female with maturity.

7 SADDLED BREAM
Oblada melanura

This species is much longer than the others in the family, growing to 30cm (1ft), with a large head and prominent eyes. It has a characteristic dark blotch at the tail juncture bordered by a white band on either side. *Ecology*: They occur in large shoals always facing into the current, where they pick at passing plankton.

1 Bump Head Bream

2 Annular Sea Bream

3 Zebra Bream

4 White Bream *(above)*

5 Two-banded Bream *(left)*

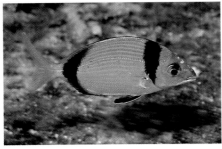

6 Striped Bream *(above)*

7 Saddled Bream *(left)*

1 PANDORA
Pagellus erythrinus

Commonly found in central and western regions, the Pandora is light tan to light brown in colour and may have some pink and bluish spots on maturity. It grows to over 35cm (1ft 2in) and is elongate with a tapering tale and rather small head. *Ecology*: It occurs on the lower reef starting off as a female and changing to male at about 16cm (6½in) in size. It feeds on small crustaceans and molluscs and has large crushing molars.

2 COW BREAM or SAUPE
Sarpa salpa

A large bream growing to 50cm (1ft 8in), it is elongate and instantly recognized by the bright golden, horizontal bands on its flanks and fleshy lips. *Ecology*: This species is always seen grazing in shoals over the algae-covered reefs. It always appears in large numbers and is constantly on the move. It is a delight for divers to see, as these large shoals always feed close to the shore.

WRASSE
Family Labridae

Wrasse are a large and diverse family and occur throughout the Mediterranean in large numbers. Most of the species are carnivorous, living on small crustaceans and molluscs and a few have very strong jaws with which to crush sea urchins. They are found around all coastlines, quite often in very large numbers. They all share common characteristics and have bodies around three times their height. They have large, fleshy, protruding lips, and prominent eyes set high on the head. They have one single low dorsal fin and short, rounded pectoral fins. A number of the juveniles of certain species act as cleaners to other fish. Most have various colour changes as they reach maturity and are often difficult to identify.

3 RAINBOW WRASSE
Coris julis

A distinctive long thin species, the Rainbow Wrasse grows to 25cm (10in) and has several colour changes in its life, usually with a mixture of horizontal stripes of many different colours from yellow to vivid orange. It may even have zig-zag bands along the flanks. It has a pointed snout and tapering tail. *Ecology*: This is a common fish feeding low over the reef and will often follow divers around as they pick on any disturbed crustaceans and worms.

4 GOLDSINNY
Ctenolabrus rupestris

A small species of wrasse, growing to 15cm (6in), it is light to golden brown in colour and has a distinctive black blotch on the top of and at the start of the tail. It has prominent buck teeth and widely set protruding eyes. *Ecology*: It is widely distributed amongst the algae close or near to the shore where it hunts in small groups.

5 BALLAN WRASSE
Labrus bergylta

This is a large brown wrasse with mottled brownish colouring and grows to 45cm (1ft 6in). It has a high convex head with steeply sloping brow and large, protruding, fleshy lips. It features an intricate network pattern around the head and lower jaw. *Ecology*: Common around coastal areas and near caverns, there are no external differences as the fish reaches maturity or between the sexes.

1 Pandora

2 Cow Bream

3 Rainbow Wrasse

4 Goldsinny

5 Ballan Wrasse

1 CUCKOO WRASSE

Labrus bimaculatus

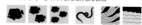

One of the most colourful of the wrasse, it grows to 35cm (1ft 2in) and is quite common around coastal areas where it prefers a rocky substrate covered with algae and many nooks and crannies to hide in. *Ecology*: At the male stage, it exhibits brilliant blue markings around the head and flanks changing to orangey red and then back to blue at the tail. The female is a golden brown with three dark markings surrounded by white at the base of the dorsal fin.

2 BROWN WRASSE

Labrus merula

This is a slender and robust fish growing to 45cm (1ft 6in). It has a moderately sized head and quite small eyes, pointed snout and thick lips. Brown to olive green in colour, the scale markings are evident and during courtship the male will develop some blue spots and blue fin edges. *Ecology*: This is quite a common, solitary fish found around rocky bottoms and near seagrass where it picks around the stones looking for food scraps.

3 GREEN WRASSE

Labrus viridus

A small wrasse, olive to golden green in colour and 15cm (6in) in length. There is some controversy over this fish, as it may actually be a juvenile form of another wrasse species, perhaps the Brown Wrasse *Labrus merula*. As yet, however, the link has not been found, and this would only happen in captivity over a long period. *Ecology*: This species likes seagrass meadows and small stony areas. It is quite timid and will quickly hide under stones if threatened.

4 CORKWING WRASSE

Symphodus melops

This species has a darker blotch across the forehead and a very varied coloration, with vertical bands of golden brown and cream. It has a high dorsal fin, dark bands at the tale, blue radiating stripes at the head and lower jaw, and grows to 30cm (1ft). *Ecology*: It lives in shallow inshore waters and is relatively uncommon. A migrant from the Atlantic, it is more at home in the western Mediterranean.

5 AXILLARY WRASSE

Symphodus mediterraneus

   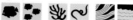

This species has a dark blotch above the lateral line at the base of the tale. It has an arched lateral line with a large head, pointed snout, prominent lips and grows to 20cm (8in). There is a prominent yellow flash at the pectoral fins around a dark blotch at the juncture of the fin. *Ecology*: The adult male will have radiating blue lines and blue markings on the fins. It prefers the zone between the sandy area and seagrass meadows.

6 LONGSNOUT WRASSE

Symphodus rostratus

This very distinct species grows to 8–15cm (3–6in) and features a concave forehead and a long, pointed snout. Variably speckled in colour, it also features a white line from its snout along the top of the back at the base of the dorsal fins. *Ecology*: It often swims in a head-down posture as it searches the algae for small shrimps, its favourite food. However, when being cleaned by other wrasse species, it hovers in a head-up position.

7 PEACOCK WRASSE

Symphodus tinca

  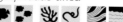

It has a prominent snout with white, fleshy lips and a dark brown band on the upper jaw radiating to the eyes. There are two or three rows of horizontal, brownish lines along the upper half of a light tan speckled body. It has an obvious pinkish patch on the gill covers. It grows to 35cm (1ft 2in). *Ecology*: This is a very common species found around seagrass meadows and all algae-covered, rocky reefs, where it feeds on small crustaceans, molluscs and worms.

1 Cuckoo Wrasse male *(above)*, female *(right)*

2 Brown Wrasse

3 Green Wrasse

4 Corkwing Wrasse

5 Axillary Wrasse

6 Longsnout Wrasse

7 Peacock Wrasse

1 ORNATE WRASSE
Thalassoma pavo

One of the most ornately coloured, this wrasse grows to 20cm (8in) and has various colour changes as it reaches maturity. Blue and olive green in colour, the juveniles exhibit a dark blotch midway down the back under the dorsal fin. *Ecology*: It loves shallow, warm coastal waters where it feeds actively on small worms and crustaceans. It is always picking around the reef and whilst it is an active predator during the day, it sleeps hidden from view, buried in sand at night.

2 PEARLY RAZORFISH
Xyrichthys novacula

This curious fish with its large, rounded head and pearly sheen to its scales is found in shallow coastal lagoons and sandy inlets away from any major water movement. Growing to 20cm (8in) it can have a light tan sheen to the scales and some radiating blue lines on the head and underside of the jay and pelvic fins on the adult males. *Ecology*: It hovers near the edge of seagrass beds and when danger threatens, this slim fish is able to dive head-first into the soft sediment to escape.

PARROTFISH
Family Scaridae

Parrotfish are distant cousins of the wrasse and where wrasse have fleshy lips, Parrotfish have a strong, calcified beak and wide molar plate. This enables them to bite chunks of coral and grind them up to get at the soft polyps within. Known to be a contributing factor in the production of sand around the offshore reefs, parrotfish are voracious eaters and are always found in small groups of perhaps ten to twenty females with one large super male.

3 PARROTFISH
Sparisoma cretense

The Mediterranean Parrotfish is always a delightful find. Uncommon in cooler western waters, it is more common east of the Maltese archipelago. The female is a brilliant mixed colour comprising a yellow ring around the eye, red snout with yellow band behind, grey head and red for the rest of the body and tail. It has another yellow patch before the tail. The males are a dull greyish blue in colour and only change sex when another predominant male has died. It grows to 50cm (1ft 8in). *Ecology*: The Parrotfish likes offshore reefs in well-aerated water and mixes well with other fish species.

DRAGONET
Family Callionymidae

4 COMMON DRAGONET
Callionymus lyra

This is a bottom-living fish with a roughly triangular-shaped head with a long lower jaw and a flattened body. The male is larger, growing to 30cm (1ft) and the female is only 20cm (8in). The eyes are large, slightly protruding and set on top of the head. It has two dorsal fins, the first on the male is very long and triangular, the second is long and rayed towards the tail. *Ecology*: During the mating season, the males change colour and have vivid blue markings around the jaw line and eyes, and along the flanks. When mating, the males display their long, colourful fin rays.

1 Ornate Wrasse

2 Pearly Razorfish

3 Parrotfish male *(left)*, female *(above)*

4 Common Dragonet

GURNARD
Family Triglidae

1 TUB GURNARD
Trigla lucerna

A large, robust fish with a stout, elongated head, the fish is principally red or pinkish-orange in colour and grows up to 75cm (2ft 6in). It has specially adapted pectoral fin rays which allow it to walk along the sandy sea floor. *Ecology*: This is the largest of the gurnard species, the young of which prefer softer muddy substrates and have the ability to dive for cover, should danger threaten. Juveniles and adults are found in small schools and they are heard to emit small grunting noises.

2 FLYING GURNARD
Dactylopterus volitans

This species grows to 50cm (1ft 8in) and is found in depths below 10m (30ft). It has variable brown, red and cream markings and the pectoral fins may be tinged with blue. Its name comes from its huge pectoral fin wing span, which allows it to 'fly' over the seabed. *Ecology*: This is a wide-ranging species and lives on sandy and muddy bottoms, usually in pairs. It is able to walk on its ventral fins.

3 STREAKED GURNARD
Trigloporus lastoviza

By far the most colourful of the species, the Streaked Gurnard is also the smallest of the species growing to only 40cm (1ft 4in). It has a mottled coloration, from tan and orange with brown blotches and has a high triangular dorsal fin. *Ecology*: When swimming normally, with its fin rays at its side, it resembles the Striped Mullet, but here the similarity ends. When it opens its pectoral fins, they display a brilliant blue in colour.

BLENNY
Family Blennidae

This is a large family of small fish which live around coastal waters and share common characteristics. They like rocky crevices and tend to perch near the entrances of them. Most have fleshy appendages above their high set eyes and, although they resemble gobies, they have shorter blunt heads, prominent lips and pectoral fins, which are more like feet. Other differing characteristics are the single or triple dorsal fin. They lie in a flexed position. They are curious fish and can be approached quite easily, but slowly.

4 TOMPOT BLENNY
Parablennius gattorugine

One of the largest and gaudiest blennies, it has a thick set body tapering to a slender tail. The forehead is high and convex and it has two very conspicuous appendages above the eyes, resembling fleshy antlers. It grows to 25cm (10in) and has seven wide, dark-brown, vertical bands on the body, which is varicoloured from brown to tan and red. *Ecology*: It is a wide-ranging species and loves to inhabit small holes with only its head protruding.

5 PIXILATED BLENNY
Parablennius pilicornis

This species grows to 12cm (5in) and can exhibit very similar colour markings to that of the Striped Blenny (*see* p.116). However, the Pixilated Blenny shows two horizontal bands, with the second band running along the base of the dorsal fin. It has variable brown vertical markings and short fleshy 'horns' above the eyes. *Ecology*: This fish enjoys algae-covered rocks and often hides in old worm holes or empty shells.

1   Tub Gurnard

2   Flying Gurnard

3   Streaked Gurnard

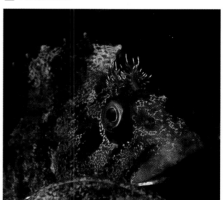

4   Tompot Blenny

5   Pixilated Blenny

1 STRIPED BLENNY
Parablennius rouxi

The Striped Blenny grows to 8cm (3in) and has a single, broad, dark strip, which traverses the length of the body from the blunt forehead, across the eyes and along to the tail juncture. It has a fairly white body with creamy spots above the longitudinal line. This species also exhibits 'horns' and these are quite long and tri-lobed. *Ecology*: It likes shallow, well-lit, warm waters and is quite at home in the surf zone as well as in harbour areas. It tends to hide in old worm or snail holes and is quite timid.

2 STAGHORN BLENNY
Parablennius zvonimiri

This species when viewed from the front resembles both the Tompot Blenny and the Striped Blenny, as it has quite long, fleshy appendages above the prominent eyes. These are longer than the Striped Blenny's and not as intricate as the Tompot Blenny's. It grows to 7cm (3in) and is quite common in the Adriatic and around the Greek islands. It is only when it comes out of its hole that the brilliant white spots along the underside of the dorsal fin can be seen. *Ecology*: This species prefers low light conditions and is more common in deeper water or at least the entrances to caverns or under rocks.

3 PEACOCK BLENNY
Salaria pavo

This is a curious-looking fish with a high-browed domed head with circular blue or white markings behind the eye and bright blue or white, thin, vertical stripes and dashes along its brown and cream flanks. Larger than some of the other species, it grows to 13cm (5in) and has a slightly down-turned mouth. *Ecology*: A rarely seen species, it enjoys seagrass meadows and algae-covered rocks. It is quite happy in a variety of

depths and is more likely to be out in the open, perched in plain sight.

4 YELLOW TRIPLEFIN
Tripterygion delasii

The appearance of the territorial, sexually mature male is what gives the species its name. Very obviously recognized by its black head and vivid yellow-golden body, it has a long snout and three obvious dorsal fins. Its adapted pelvic fins are also black. It grows to 9cm (3½in) and is widely spread throughout the region. *Ecology*: It likes to perch at curious angles on algae-encrusted rocks and is able to move quite quickly when approached. The species is very territorial and will actively defend its territory against all other males.

5 SMALL TRIPLEFIN
Tripterygion melanurus

The Small Triplefin has three distinct dorsal fins and a black blotch surrounded by white at the tail and another white blotch between the second and third dorsal fins. The pectoral fins are speckled white and the species grow to only 5cm (2in). *Ecology*: This species of blenny has many different colour forms and can be quite difficult to identify. It lives amidst the fuzzy, algae-covered rocks and likes very shallow, warm, well-lit water.

6 SMALL TRIPLEFIN
Tripterygion melanurus minor

Sometimes referred to as *Tripterygion xanthosoma*, this small blenny is almost identical in nature and habit to its cousin, except for the coloration. More readily found in the Adriatic around Croatia, this subspecies appears to be spreading throughout the Mediterranean and may well be considered as a full species. *Ecology*: This species is determined by the lack of the distinct black spot or dash on the tail.

1   Striped Blenny

2   Staghorn Blenny

3   Peacock Blenny

4   Yellow Triplefin

5   Small Triplefin

6   Small Triplefin *T. melanurus minor*

STARGAZER
Family Uraniscopidae

1 STARGAZER
Uranoscopus scaber

Very difficult to detect, this large, rotund fish grows to around 35cm (1ft 2in) and is often found in shallow water where it lies buried in the sand. The top of the body is fairly flat and has a low dorsal fin far down the back, reaching the tail, which it folds flat when hiding. It has large, up-turned eyes and an even larger up-turned mouth with large, overlapping teeth. *Ecology*: It has a fleshy appendage attached to its lower lip, which it waves about to attract prey. A fairly timid fish, it will scuttle off in short bursts of speed if annoyed.

WEAVERFISH
Family Trachinidae

2 GREATER WEAVERFISH
Trachinus draco

Similar in shape to stargazers, weaverfish are longer and slimmer, but use the same techniques for catching prey. They grow to around 40cm (1ft 4in) long and have a hinged, down-turned mouth. Tan to lightish blue on the flanks, the back of the head is mottled. *Ecology*: The first dorsal fin has three adapted spines, which it uses for defence. These spines are venomous, with poison glands at the base.

3 STREAKED WEAVERFISH
Trachinus radiatus

The coloration of this fish tends to be more pronounced, almost like leopard skin along the top of its back and flanks. The sting is equally as painful and should be treated with potassium permanganate and/or bathing the wound in as hot water as possible. *Ecology:* The principal difference is that the Greater Weaverfish usually hides in the sand with only its eyes and mouth visible. The Streaked always sits high on top of the sand.

GOBIES
Family Gobiidae

Gobies have two dorsal fins and hold themselves quite rigidly when at rest. The pelvic fins are generally modified into a sucker disc, which keeps the fish securely in place whilst balanced precariously on some underhanging rock ledge. Most gobies are bottom dwellers and whilst they live in a common habitat are a wide and diversely coloured species with different habits.

4 ANEMONE GOBY
Gobius bucchichii

This goby grows to 10cm (4in) long and is a varied colour of pale cream with numerous dotted patterns about the head and body. It prefers to live on the sandy seabed, always near a rocky crevice. It feeds on small crustaceans and worms and is an active daytime as well as night-time feeder. *Ecology*: This is the only species of goby (that we know of) in the Mediterranean which has a relationship with anemones, namely the Snakelocks Anemone *Anemonia sulcata*.

1 Stargazer *(above)*

2 Greater Weaverfish *(right)*; (inset: hidden in the sand)

3 Streaked Weaverfish

4 Anemone Goby

1 GIANT GOBY

Gobius cobitus

The largest goby in the eastern Atlantic and Mediterranean, the Giant Goby grows to 27cm (11in) long and is found as far east as the shores of the Black Sea. It is a variable grey to cream and black in colour and has prominent eyes and thick, fleshy lips. It feeds on algae as well as small crustaceans, worms and molluscs, and has powerful jaws. *Ecology*: The spread of this fish is quite remarkable as it was originally thought to have migrated into the Mediterranean from the Atlantic. It has now extended its range further and expanded from the Mediterranean into the northern Red Sea via the Suez Canal. It tends to lie in wait in a hole, waiting for its meal to swim by. It reaches sexual maturity at two to three years of age and lives for up to ten years. Unlike other Mediterranean gobies, and probably the reason for its success, it not only eats benthic invertebrates and fish, but also algae, and it is tolerant of not only light pollution but also fresh water.

2 RED-LIPPED GOBY

Gobius cruenatus

This species grows to only 18cm (7in) and is instantly recognized by its red lips. It has an elongated, circular body, large head with black sensory spots and an unbranched tentacle over each nostril. It has an overall blotched dark colour appearance. *Ecology*: It enjoys low light conditions and prefers to stay within reach of a rocky overhang or rock to hide under should danger threaten. It is quite easily recognized.

3 SAND GOBY

Gobius geniporus

This small species grows to 16cm (6in) and is perhaps the most common of all the gobies encountered. Found on the seabed on sand and around seagrass meadows; it can occur in large numbers. It has excellent camouflage, having similar markings to the speckles of the sand and gravel habitat it prefers. *Ecology*: It may have good camouflage, but it is too curious to keep away and when you are photographing other sedentary creatures, many of the these gobies will come and look at what is going on.

4 BLACK GOBY

Gobius niger

This is a large goby growing to over 15cm (6in) and it quite enjoys harbours and brackish waters, where it is at home in estuaries, coastal lagoons and sea lochs. Sexually mature at two years of age, the territorial males and juveniles are jet black (hence the name) and have a life span of five years. The Black Goby is widely distributed from Norway to the Canary Islands and Mauritania as well as through the Mediterranean into the furthest reaches of the Adriatic and the Black Sea. *Ecology*: It is very territorial in nature and is locally common on all sandy seabeds, preferring the shelter of nearby reefs and seagrass meadows.

5 LEOPARD SPOTTED GOBY

Thorogobius ephippiatus

This is another very distinctive goby and cannot be confused with any other species. It grows to 13cm (5in) and is covered in dark purplish blotches on a pinkish-blue background. Widely distributed, it can be found from the Black Sea to Northern Norway and the Canary Islands. *Ecology*: Quite a sociable fish, it tends to be found in pairs or small groups, their heads usually aligned back towards a rocky recess where they quickly dart for cover if disturbed or threatened. This species prefers low light conditions and a soft substrate and, consequently, it is more commonly seen in caves and caverns. It is an active predator at night, feeding on small worms and crustaceans.

1 Giant Goby   **2** Red-lipped Goby

3 Sand Goby *(above)*   **4** Black Goby *(below)*   **5** Leopard Spotted Goby *(bottom)*

CODFISH
Family Gadidae

These have a cylindrical body and a relatively large head. Whilst many of the species hunt in large packs in open waters, the two species represented here are both shy creatures, preferring low light. They are soft rayed fish possessing fleshy barbels of some sort, have two or three dorsal fins and one or two anal fins.

1 SHORE ROCKLING
Gaidropsarus vulgaris

This species is usually a uniform reddish-brown in colour and has three obvious fleshy appendages, two on the snout and the other under the chin. It grows to 50cm (1ft 8in) and is a solitary living fish. *Ecology*: It prefers low light and will inhabit deeper caverns and crevices, venturing out at night to feed. Very shy, it will soon scuttle away should it be disturbed.

2 FORKBEARD
Phycis phycis

This is a very distinctive shy species of the cod family. It has a long barbel under the chin and an even longer one which is split into two, at the base of the underside of the jaw. It has another two protuberances at the underside of the gill flaps. It is coloured a light tan with a creamy underbelly and grows to 25cm (10in). *Ecology*: This species is an active night hunter, feeding on small crustaceans, worms and fish fry. It is light-sensitive and always keeps well away from strong sunlight, preferring caves and deep crevices.

FLOUNDER
Family Bothidae

Flounders or flatfish are highly specialized fish which live principally on the seabed. Their bodies have adapted to this life by the eye on the underside of the head moving around the body to be on the top. In some cases the topside pectoral fin is much longer, acting as a mating signal or sail. The body is ringed with both the dorsal and pelvic fin. All are carnivorous, feeding on molluscs, worms and crustaceans which are found in the same habitat.

3 WIDE-EYED FLOUNDER
Bothus podas

This flatfish grows to 45cm (1ft 6in) and is quite cylindrical in shape. Its topside skin markings are a mottled brown with circular, creamy spots and blotches. The eyes are quite wide apart and obliquely set. The right-hand side (underside or offside) is creamy white. *Ecology*: This bottom-dwelling fish is fairly common on flat sandy areas in lagoons and estuaries. It tends to hide under the sand with only its eyes showing and although it is common, it is difficult to spot unless disturbed accidentally.

4 PLAICE
Pleuronectes platessa

More common in the western Mediterranean, this fish is an Atlantic migrant, with distinctive red spots on a brown topside body. It grows to 1m (3ft 3in). The eyes are raised and alongside each other, and it is much more of a diamond shape. *Ecology*: This is a commercially harvested species and much sought after in the marketplace. It frequently enters brackish water and is quite approachable.

1 Shore Rockling

2 Forkbeard

3 Wide-eyed Flounder

4 Plaice

1 TURBOT
Psetta maxima

This is one of the largest flatfish to be found in the region and ranges from the Black Sea into the Atlantic. A creature of deeper water, it may be encountered around deeper wrecks. It can grow up to 1m (3ft 3in) and has wide-set, protruding eyes. The topside skin has no scales and is covered by rough bony tubercles. *Ecology*: This is a bottom-dwelling species and likes company, quite often found in small groups. It can live to over twenty years of age. It spawns in July and August. The four egg sacs are always carried in the left-hand side of the body with a large cavity on both top and bottom.

TURTLES

2 HAWKSBILL TURTLE
Eretmochelys imbricata

This is certainly an endangered species in the Mediterranean. The nesting beaches are under threat of tourist development. Often caught in trawl nets, the turtle feeds on jellyfish, sponges and some algae. It has a hawk-like beak and overlapping bony plates along its back, unlike the Green Turtle. Growing to 1.20m (4ft), the Hawksbill Turtle is more commonly seen in the western Mediterranean, where it migrates from the Atlantic. The marine museum, Aula del Mar, in Malaga cares for wounded individuals and these can be observed by the public while the turtles are in care.

3 GREEN TURTLE
Chelonia mydas

This turtle was once very common in central and eastern regions of the Mediterranean, but it is now more confined to the Greek islands and Turkish coasts, where there are still protected breeding beaches. However, many turtles are caught each year as a by-catch from drift netting and it is now considered endangered. This species has non-overlapping body plates, whereas the Hawksbill has overlapping body plates, and it is smaller at up to 1m (3ft 3in) long. The other obvious difference is that there are only two plate sections on the forehead of the Green Turtle and four distinct plate sections on the head of the Hawksbill Turtle.

DOLPHINS

4 BOTTLE-NOSED DOLPHIN
Tursiops truncatus

This is the most commonly encountered dolphin in the region and pods of them can be found in many areas, such as at Gibraltar, Sicily and around the Greek islands. It has a nice, friendly face with a long snout and high forehead, and grows up to 4m (13ft) long. This species enjoys riding the bow wave of fast boats, and this is probably the best way that tourists will enjoy it in the Mediterranean.

1 Turbot

2 Hawksbill Turtle

3 Green Turtle

4 Bottle-nosed Dolphin

GLOSSARY

Aggregation: individuals gathered together in a loose group. Can apply to fish or to attached animals.

Anal fin: single fin running along the underside of a fish, from the anal opening towards the tail.

Benthic: dwelling on the seabed, either attached or unattached.

Colony/colonial: animal that consists of numerous similar or identical 'units' (e.g. polyps) that are linked together to form the complete organism.

Commensal: relationship in which two species live in close physical association, and are dependent on each other for some function or other.

Dorsal fin: fin running along the top of the body in the mid-line; it may be single or split into two or three separate sections.

Hermaphrodite: individual that contains both ovaries and testes in its body. These may be functional at the same time, or the animal may function first as one sex and then the other.

Ectoparasite: animal that lives on the outside of another, and is dependent on it for its nutrition (e.g. it attaches to the skin and feeds on blood).

Invertebrates: animals without backbones.

Lessepsian: all species of marine life that have travelled through to the Mediterranean from the Red Sea are known as Lessepsian migrants after the engineer's name, Ferdinand De Lesseps.

Omnivorous/omnivores: animals with a diet consisting of a mixture of plant and animal material.

Herbivorous/herbivores: animals that feed on plants, such as algae and seagrasses.

Plankton: plants (phytoplankton) or animals (zooplankton) that float in the water column and are moved by ocean currents. Mainly microscopic, but includes larger organisms, such as jellyfish.

Pectoral fins: pair of fins located one each side of the body, just behind the head.

Pelagic: living and swimming in the water column, rather than close to or on the seabed.

Pelvic fins: pair of fins located on the underside of the fish, usually beneath the pectoral fins.

Predator: animal that hunts and feeds on other animals.

Symbiotic: relationship in which two (or more) species live together and benefit each other in one or more ways.

Territory: living, feeding or breeding area that is actively defended from intruders by the inhabitant(s).

INDEX

Abalone 62
Acanthella acuta 32, 34
Acetabularia mediterranea 26
Actinothoe sphryodeta 46
Adamsia carciniapados 46, 76
Aeolid, Migrating 66
Aequipecten opercularis 60
Aglophenia spp. 38
Aiptasia mutabilis 46
Alcyonium acaule 44
    palmatum 44
Alga, Killer 7, 18, 28
algae 26
    brown 32
    green 26
    red 30
Alicia mirabilis 15, 46
Amberjack, Great 100
    Mediterranean 100
Anemone, Berried 15, 46
    Cloak 46
    Dahlia 48
    Daisy 48
    firework 42
    Fireworks 48
    Golden 48
    Hermit 46
    Jewel 48
    Snakelocks 46, 48, 76, 118
    Trumpet 46
Anemonia sulcata 46, 76, 118

Anglerfish 94
Anguilla anguilla 90
Antedon mediterranea 78
Anthias anthias 96
Aphrodita aculeata 54
Aplidium conicum 82
Aplysia fasciata 66
    punctata 66
Apogon imberbis 98
Apogonidae 98
Arbacia lixula 80
Ascidians 82
Ascidiella aspersa 84
Astroides calycularis 50
Astropecten irregularis 80
Atherina hepsetus 104
Atherinidae 104
Aurelia aurita 40
Axinella canabina 34
    damicornis 34
    polypoides 34
    verrucosa 34

Barnacle, Goose 72
    Star 70
Barracuda 100
Bass, Sea 96
Blennidae 114
Blenny, Peacock 116
    Pixilated 114
    Staghorn 116
    Striped 114, 116
    Tompot 114, 116
Bogue 104

Bonellia viridis 54
Boops boops 104
Bothidae 122
Bothus podas 122
Bream 104
    Annular Sea 106
    Bump Head 106
    Cow 108
    Saddled 106
    Striped 106
    Two-banded 106
    White 106
    Zebra 106
Brittlestar, Black 78
    Fragile 78
    Long-Armed 78
Bryozoans 50
Buccinulum corneum 60

Caberea boryi 50, 52
Cactus, Sea 28
Calcinus tubularis 76
Calliactis parasitica 46, 74
Callionymidae 112
Callionymus lyra 112
Caranx crysos 100
    hippos 100
Carcharias taurus 86
Carcharinus obscurus 20
Cardinalfish 98
Carpet Shell, Golden 64
    Smooth 64
Carrangidae 100
Caryophyllia smithii 50

Cassiopeia 40
Caulerpa mexicana 28
    prolifera 28
    racemosa 28, 68
    racemosa var. occidentalis 28
    taxifolia 7–8, 11, 18, 28
Caulerpa, Common 28
Caulerpa, Creeping 28
Centracanthidae 104
Centrostephanus longispinus 13, 16, 82
Cephalapods 58
Cereus pedunculatus 48
Cerianthus membranaceus 48
Cerith, Mediterranean 60
Cerithium vulgatum 60
Chandrilla nucula 34
Charonia tritonis 62
Chelonia mydas 124
Chiton 60
Chiton olivaceus 60
Chlorophyta 26
Chromis 8, 20, 102, 104
Chromis chromis 8, 20, 102
Chthalamus stellatus 70
Ciona 84
Ciona intestinalis 84
Cladocora caespitosa 50
Clathrina 34
Clathrina clathrus 34
    coriacea 34
Clavelina dellavaliei 84
    lepadiformis 84

nana 84
Cliona viridis 34
Cnidarians 38
Codfish 122
Codium bursa 28
  vermilara 28
Codium, Finger 28
  Purse 28
Comber 98
  Black Tail 98
  Painted 98
Condylactis aurantiaca 48
Cone Shell, Mediterranean
  62
Conger conger 90
Conus mediterraneus 62
Coral, Cup 50
  Dark Solitary 50
  Deer Horn 52
  False 52
  False Red 44
  Frond 52
  Lace 50
  Mat 50
  Precious 42
  Red 13, 42
  Rough 30
  Star 50
  Yellow Cup 50
Corallina elongata 30
Corallium rubrum 13, 42
Coris julis 108
Corynactis viridis 48
Coryphella pedata 66, 68
Corystes cassivelaunus 76
Coscinasterias tenuispina
  80
Cothyloriza tubercolata 40
Cotton Spinner 82
Cowrie, Mediterranean 62
  Spotted 62
Crab, Anemone Spider 76
  Common Spider 78
  Hairy Hermit 76
  Masked 76
  Prideaux's Hermit 76
  Red Hermit 74
  Red Spider 78
  Sedentary Hermit 76
  Spiny Spider 76
  Sponge 76
  Striped Hermit 76
Crambe crambe 36, 64
Cratena peregrina 66
Cribinopsis crassa 48, 72
Crinoids 78
Crustaceans 70
Crystal Tips 68
Ctenolabrus rupestris 108
Cucumber, Tubular 82
  White Spot 82
Cuttlefish, Common 60
Cymodocea 64
Cymodocea nodosa 26
Cyprea lurida 62
  spurca 62

Dactylopterus volitans 114
Damselfish 20, 102
Dardanus calidus 74
Dasyatis pastinaca 88
Dead Men's Fingers 44

Dendrodoa spp. 84
Dendrodoris limbata 68
Dentex dentex 104
  gibbosus 106
Dentex, Common 104
Dicentrarchus labrax 96
Dictyota dichotoma 32
Diozone violacea 84
Diplodus annularis 106
  cervinus 106
  sargus 106
  vulgaris 106
Discodoris atromaculata
  36, 70
Dogfish, Lesser-spotted 86
Dolphin, Bottle-nosed 124
Dorid, White Lined 68
Doriopsilla pelseneri 68
Doris, Leathery 70
  Spotted 36, 70
  Tri-colour 68
Dragonet, Common 112
Dromia personata 76
Drum 102
Dyscidea fragilis 36

Echinaster sepositus 80
Echinocardium cordatum 80
Echinoderms 78
Eel, Common 90
  Conger 90
  Moray 90
  Serpent 90
Eledone moschata 58
Elysia 68
Elysia viridis 68
Epinephelus caninus 96
  costae 96
  marginatus 7, 13, 96
Eretmochelys imbricata 124
Eudendrium 66, 68
  rameum 40
Eunicella cavolinii 42
  singularis 42
  verrucosa 42

Fan, Sea 28
Fern, Sea 32, 38
File Shell, Spiny 62
Filograna implexa 56
Fir, Sea 40
Flabellina affinis 68
Flatworm, Brown 54
  Pink 54
Flounder 122
Flounder, Wide-eyed 122
Forkbeard 122
Forked Ribbons 32
Frondipora verrucósa 52

Gadidae 122
Gaidropsarus vulgaris 122
Galathea strigosa 74
Gastropods 60
Goatfish 102
Gobies 118
Gobiidae 118
Gobius bucchichii 118
  cobitus 120
  cruenatus 120
  geniporus 120
  niger 120

Goby, Anemone 118
  Black 120
  Giant 120
  Leopard Spotted 120
  Red-lipped 120
  Sand 120
Godiva banyulensis 68
Goldsinny 108
Gorgonians 42–4
Grass, Neptune 11, 26
Green Tongue 54
Grouper, Canine 96
  Dusky 7, 13, 96
  Goldblotch 96
  Striped 96
Gurnard, Flying 114
  Streaked 114
  Tub 114
Gymnangium montagui 40

Halimeda tuna 28
Haliotis lamellosa 62
Halocinthya papillosa 84
Halophila 26
Halophila stipulacea 26
Halopteris scoporici 32
Herbstia condyliata 76
Hermodice carunculata 16,
  54
Hexacorallia 46–8
Himantura uarnak 88
Hippocampus spp. 13
  ramulosus 92
Holothuria forskåli 82
  polii 82
  tubulosa 82
Homarus gammarus 74
Hound, Nurse 88
  Smooth 86
Hydroid, Encrusting 52
Hydroids 38–40
Hypselodoris elegans 68
  picta 68
  tricolor 68
  valenciennesi 68
  webbi 68

Inachus phalangium 76
Ircinia spinosa 36

Jack, Crevalle 100
Jacks 100
Jania 30
Jania rubens 30 ·
Janolus cristatus 68
Jellyfish 40
  Bell 40
  Fried Egg 40
  Luminescent 15, 40
  Moon 40

Labridae 108
Labrus bergylta 108
  bimaculatus 110
  merula 110
  viridus 110
Lady Godiva 68
Lementina arenoria 62
Lepas anserifera 72
Leptosammia pruvoti 50
Lima lima 62
Limpet, Giant 21

Lissa chiragra 78
Lithognathus mormyrus
  106
Lithophyllum lichonoides
  30
Lizardfish 92
Lobster, Common 74
  Long-Clawed Squat 74
  Small Locust 74
  Spiny 74
  Strident Squat 74
Loligo vulgaris 60
Lophidae 94
Lophius piscatorius 94
Lophogorgia sarmentosa 44

Macrohamphodidae 92
Macrohamphosus scolopax
  92
Maja crispata 78
Marthasterias glacialis 80
Meagre, Brown 102
Mermaid's Cup 26
Molluscs 58
Monachus monachus 13
Moss, Rhodophyta 30
Mother of Pearl 13
Muglidae 102
Mullet, Boxlip 102
  Grey 102
  Striped 102, 114
Mullidae 102
Mullus surmuletus 102
Munida rugosa 74
Muraena helena 90
Mussel, Common 64
  Giant Fan 18
Mustelus mustelus 86
Myriapora truncata 52
Mytilus edulis 64
Myxicola infundibulum 56

Neptune's Lace 52
Nudibranch, Four-lined 70
  Purple 66, 68
  White-tipped 66
Nymphon Amethysteus 70

Oblada melanura 106
Octocorallia 44
Octopus macropus 58
  vulgaris 60
Octopus, Common 58, 60
  Musky 58
  White-spotted 58
Odontaspis ferox 20
Oedalechilus labeo 102
Ophidiaster ophidianus 80
Ophiocomino nigra 78
Ophioderma longicauda 78
Ophiothrix fragilis 78
Ophisunus serpens 90
Oscarella lobularis 36
Oyster, Winged 64

Padina pavonica 32
Pagarus anachoretus 76
  cuanensis 76
  prideaux 46, 76
Pagellus erythrinus 108
Palaemon elegans 72
  serratus 72

Palinurus elephas 74
Pandora 108
Paphia aurea 64
Parablennius gattorugine
   114
   pilicornis 114
   rouxi 116
   zvonimiri 116
Paracentrotus lividus 82
Paramuricea clavata 42
Paramysis helleri 72
Parazoanthus axinellae 48
Parerythropodium
   coralloides 44
Parrotfish 112
Peacock's Tail 32
Pelagia noctiluca 15, 40
Pen Shell, Noble 64
   Rough 64
Pennaria disticha 16
Pentapora fascialis 52
Periclimenes amethysteus
   48, 72
Petrosia ficiformis 36, 70
Peyssonnelia squamaria
   30
Phaeophyta 32
Phycis phycis 122
Phyllangia mouchezii 50
Physalia physalis 15
Picarel 104
Pinna nobilis 13, 18, 64
   rudis 64
Pipefish 92
Pitar rudis 64
Plaice 122
Platydoris argo 70
Plesionica narval 72
Pleurobranchs 66
Pleuronectes platessa 122
Polycera quadrilineata 70
Polycirrus spp. 56
Pomacentridae 102
Pomatocerous triqueter 56
Porifera 32
Portuguese Man-of-War 15
Posidonia oceanica 11, 13,
   26
Prionace glauca 86
Prosthecerraeus giesbrechtii
   54
Protula tubularia 56, 58
Psetta maxima 124
Pseudolithophyllum
   expansum 30
Pteria hirundo 64

Raja clavata 88
   miraletus 90
Ray, Electric 90
   Four-eyed 90
   Thornback 88
Razorfish, Pearly 112
Red Star 80
Rhizostoma pulmo 40
Rockfish, Great 94
   Small 94
Rockling, Shore 122
Runner, Blue 100

Sabella pavonina 56
Salaria pavo 116

Sargassum vulgare 32
Sargassum, Common 32
Sarpa salpa 108
Saupe 108
Scallop, Queen 60
   Rock 64
Scaridae 112
Schizomavella mamillata
   52
Sciaena umbra 102
Sciaenidea 102
Scorpaena notata 94
   porcus 94
   scrofa 94
Scorpaenidae 94
Scorpionfish, Brown 94
Scyliorhinus canicula 86
   stellaris 86
Scyllaris arctus 74
Sea Cucumbers 82
Sea Fan, Red 42
   Warty 42
   White 42
Sea Feather 40
Sea Fingers 44
Sea Grass, Posidonia 13
Sea Hare, Giant 66
   Small 66
Sea Horse, Long-snout 92
Sea Lemon 68
Sea Mat 30
Sea Mouse 54
Sea Nettle 16
Sea Pen, Common 44
   Round 44
Sea Potato 80, 84
Sea Rose 19, 30
Sea Slug, Ceuta 70
   Elegant 68
Sea Spider 70
Sea Urchin, Black 80
   Crowned 13
   Rock 80, 82
   Violet 82
Seagrass 26
Seal, Monk 13
Seaperch, Swallowtail 96
Seaweed, Red 30
Securiflustra securifrons 52
Sepia officinalis 60
Seriola carpenteri 100
   dumerili 100
Serpula vermicularis 56,
   58
Serranidae 96
Serranus atricauda 98
   cabrilla 98
   scriba 98
Sertella beaniana 19
   septentrionalis 52
Shark, Dusky 20
   Angel 88
   Blue 86
   Ragged-tooth 20, 86
   Sand Tiger 86
Shrimp, Amethyst 48, 72
   Cleaner 72
   Common 72
   Elegant 72
   Opossum 72
   Unicorn 72
Smelt, Sand 104

Smittina cervicornis 52
Snail, Tube 62
   Umbrella 66
Snipefish 92
Sparidae 104
Sparisoma cretense 112
Spatangus purpureus 80
Sphaerechinus granularis
   82
Sphaerococcus coronpifolius
   30
Sphyraena sphyraena 100
   viridensis 100
Sphyraenidae 100
Spicara maena 104
Spirastrella cunctatrix 36
Spirographis spallanzani
   58
Spondylus gaederopus 64
Sponge, Black 36
   Boring 34
   Branching Tube 34
   Breadcrumb 36
   Greek Bath 36
   Large Encrusting 38
   Lobed 36
   Orange 36
   Oyster 36
   Pink Cave 36
   Potato 34
   Purse 38
   Spiky 32
   Yellow Branching 34
   Yellow Tube 34
Spongia officinalis 36
Spurdog 88
Squalus acanthias 88
Squatina squatina 88
Squid, Calamari 60
Starfish, Burrowing 80
   Feather 78
   Irregular 80
   Long-limb 80
   Spiny 80
Stargazer 16, 118
Stenopus spinosus 72
Stingray, Common 88
Stone Weed 30
Suberites domuncula 38
Sycon ciliatum 38
Sygnathidae 92
Sygnathus acus 92
Symphodus mediterraneus
   110
Symphodus melops 110
   rostratus 110
   tinca 110
Synodontidae 92
Synodus saurus 92

Tambja ceuta 70
Thalassoma pavo 112
Thorogobius ephippiatus
   120
Thunnus thynnus 12
Torpedo marmorata 90
Trachinidae 118
Trachinus draco 16, 118
   radiatus 118
Trigla lucerna 114
Triglidae 114
Trigloporus lastoviza 114

Triplefin, Small 116
   Yellow 116
Tripterygion delasii 116
   melanurus 116
   melanurus minor 116
   xanthosoma 116
Trumpet, Triton 62
Trunculariopis trunculus 66
Tuna, Common 12
Tunicate, Ball 84
   Bluestriped Light Bulb
   84
   Conical 82
   Glass Bell 84
   Light Bulb 84
Turbot 124
Tursiops truncatus 124
Turtle, Green 124
   Hawksbill 124

Udotea petiolata 28
Umbraculum
   mediterraneum 66
Uraniscopidae 118
Uranoscopus scaber 16,
   118
Urchin, Long-spined 82
   Purple Heart 80

Venus verrucosa 66
Venus, Warty 66
Veretillum cynomorium 44
Verongia aerophoba 34
Virgularia mirabilis 44

Weaverfish, Greater 118
   Streaked 118
Whelk 60
   Truncated 66
Whipray, Honeycomb 88
Worm, Bearded Fire 54
   Delicate Coral 56
   Fire 16
   Inquisitive Tube 56
   Mud 56
   Peacock 56
   Small Tube 56
   Spiral Tube 58
   Variable Tube 58
   White Tufted 56
Worms, Annelid 54
   Errant 54
   Polychaete 54
   Sedentary 56
Wrack, Branching Horn 52
Wrasse, Axillary 110
   Ballan 108
   Brown 110
   Corkwing 110
   Cuckoo 110
   Green 110
   Longsnout 110
   Ornate 112
   Peacock 110
   Rainbow 108

Xyrichthys novacula 112

Yungia aurantiaca 54

Zoanthid, Golden 48